RAD RIDES

RAD RIDES
THE BEST BMX BIKES
OF ALL TIME

INTERCITY, GAVIN LUCAS AND STUART ROBINSON

LAURENCE KING PUBLISHING

VANS

LAURENCE KING

Published in 2012 by
Laurence King Publishing Ltd
361–373 City Road
London EC1V 1LR
Tel: +44 20 7841 6900
Fax: +44 20 7841 6910
email: enquiries@laurenceking.com
www.laurenceking.com

A catalogue record for this book is available from the British Library.

ISBN 13: 978 1 85669 726 2

Design: Intercity
www.intercitystudio.com
Picture research: Ida Riveros

Printed in China

CONTENTS

INTRODUCTION

If someone tells you they have never wanted a BMX, they're probably lying. There is something about a BMX that appeals to kids, adults, cyclists and, more often than not, those involved in visual creativity. BMX bikes are iconic; they have a visual allure that is hard to quantify. Olympic gold-medal-winning cyclist Chris Hoy, who won three gold medals at the 2008 Olympic Games in Beijing, China, started his cycling career on a BMX. How did he get into BMX racing? He saw a BMX in the movie *E.T.* and had to get one. BMX bikes can have that effect on people.

It all began in the mid 1960s when bicycle manufacturer Schwinn released its Sting Ray model – a bike proportioned less like a road bike and more like a motocross (MX) motorcycle – so young kids could emulate their MX heroes. This was a response to the growing popularity of motocross (off-road motorcycle racing) in the United States at the time.

In 1969 one of the very first recorded bicycle motocross (BMX) races took place in Santa Monica, California, when teenage motocross rider and park attendant Ronald Mackler organized a race at the request of local kids. In 1970 Scot Breithaupt, a 13-year-old motocross racer from Long Beach, California, established a track in his area and not only organized races, but also founded the first sanctioning body of sorts for BMX – the Bicycle United Motocross Society (B.U.M.S.).

BMX was taking hold. The following year, 1971, is considered pivotal in BMX history. A motocross documentary called *On Any Sunday* (dir. Bruce Brown) arrived in cinemas across the United States and, while the film focused entirely on motorcycle racing, the opening sequence showed kids cycling customized Schwinns and hand-built bikes around a sun-drenched dirt track.

Every kid who saw the documentary wanted to get a bike and race on a dirt track or wheelie down their street. Even though the idea did not yet have a name, practically every boy in the United States wanted to ride a bicycle like it was a motorbike. They wanted to BMX.

By 1975, as the popularity of the sport took hold, manufacturers began creating bikes specially designed for it. This was the year that BMX held its first professional race and the 20-inch wheel was introduced as the specific-to-BMX size wheel – a standard that still exists today. Schwinn's 1975 Scrambler model is a great example of an early production BMX bike. However, new companies (such as SE Racing) were beginning to emerge that were interested in experimenting with lighter materials and new welding techniques to create bicycles specially built for dirt-track racing. Off the track, other bike manufacturers saw an opportunity to cash in on the BMX craze. The Kawasaki BX200, which first appeared in the mid 1970s, is one of several factory-built bikes that looked like a motocross bike. It looked the part, and even won races (see page 20), but advancing bike technology soon meant that heavy bikes, complete with their 'monoshock' suspension systems, quickly became destined to rust away in sheds as lighter, stronger and faster bikes emerged.

In 1977 the American Bicycle Association (ABA) was formed as a national sanctioning body for the growing sport of BMX racing. In 1981 the International BMX Federation was founded and the first World Championships were held the following year. BMX was integrated into the *Union Cycliste Internationale* in 1993 and in 2003 the International Olympic Committee made BMX a full medal Olympic sport for the 2008 Olympic Games in Beijing, China. Latvian Maris Štrombergs and Anne-Caroline Chausson of France were crowned the first male and female Olympic BMX champions. Many riders who started out racing BMX bikes have gone on to achieve greatness in other cycling disciplines, such as the Australian Jared Graves, the aforementioned British Olympian Chris Hoy and fellow British team rider Jamie Staff.

Others involved in BMX have gone on to found manufacturing companies. Gary Turner, founder of GT Bicycles along with Richard Long, got into frame making because his son was a BMX racer in the early 1970s. Bob Haro, widely regarded as the pioneer of freestyle BMX riding, founded Haro Bikes – the first manufacturing company to produce BMX bikes specifically for performing freestyle tricks. Matt Hoffman, who took vert ramp riding to dizzying new heights (literally) as a teenager in the late 1980s and early 1990s, now owns his own bike company. So does Dave Mirra, another famed vert rider who has won medals in every X Games that he has taken part in since the games' inception in 1995. Today, there are dozens of BMX manufacturers, hundreds of different models of production bikes have been devised and manufactured over the years, and riders continue to custom build their own bikes to suit their chosen discipline or style of BMX riding.

BMX has come a long way since its humble origins on dirt tracks in California in the late 1960s and early 1970s, and the associated culture is vast. *Rad Rides: The Best BMX Bikes of All Time* charts the development of BMX from the sport's early days through to the present. The bikes themselves act as the sport's DNA, adapting to and reflecting its history through the trends of racing, freestyle and everything that has followed.

Due to the vast amount of BMX bikes produced and built since the sport's inception, the selection of bikes included here should not be considered definitive. There are, without a doubt, dozens of amazing bikes – both factory production bikes and custom builds – that are omitted from these pages. However, these bikes have been selected for inclusion on account of their design, their look, and their place in BMX history. Some of the bikes shown are well-worn, having been ridden hard by their owners for years. Others are beautiful, sculptural works of art, built but never ridden and displayed in their owners' homes as keepsakes. These bikes might recall good times past or realize a childhood dream of having a particular, previously unobtainable model. In this book we remove the riders from the picture and let the bikes themselves take centre stage. Where possible we have listed the component parts that make up each bike, although not every nut and bolt can be accounted for, particularly as the older bikes are approaching 40 years old.

A huge thank you to all the riders and collectors that have taken the time to photograph their bikes and submit them to be featured here in *Rad Rides*.

OLYMPIC GOLD-MEDAL-WINNING CYCLIST CHRIS HOY... STARTED HIS CYCLING CAREER ON A BMX BIKE. HOW DID HE GET INTO BMX RACING? HE SAW A BMX IN THE MOVIE *E.T.* AND HAD TO GET ONE. BMX BIKES CAN HAVE THAT EFFECT ON PEOPLE.

Schwinn Sting Ray, submitted by Marc Seemann.
Schwinn launched its Sting Ray model in 1963. With its relatively small wheels, enormous handlebars and banana seat, it was meant to echo the form of motorbikes popular at the time. This is the bike kids were racing when bicycle motocross was born in the late 1960s and early 1970s.

The Schwinn Scrambler, submitted by Michael Gamstetter.

THE MULTIPLE DISCIPLINES OF BMX

IT WAS RACING THAT STARTED IT ALL, BUT THE OTHER OPTION FOR BMX RIDERS IS TO RIDE FREESTYLE, WHICH CAN BE SPLIT INTO FIVE DIFFERENT DISCIPLINES THAT ALL SHARE A COMMON GOAL: TO SHOW SKILL AND CREATIVITY ON A BMX BIKE. THERE ARE NO HARD AND FAST RULES.

// RACING

It all started with racing and now, of course, BMX racing is an Olympic sport. In the Olympics, eight riders compete in each race heat and the track is about 350–370 metres (a quarter of a mile) long with jumps, banked corners and other obstacles. The fastest rider wins – it's as simple as that.

// FLATLAND

To ride flatland, no ramps or obstacles are needed. All a flatland rider requires is a smooth flat surface, such as a car park or basketball court. Tricks are performed by spinning and balancing in a variety of body and bike positions. Flatland bikes tend to have a shorter wheelbase than other freestyle bikes. This means it requires less effort to make the bike spin or balance on one wheel. Flatland frames are usually reinforced because riders stand on them and put them under a whole range of stresses beyond merely sitting on the seat. The sprocket on a flatland rider's bike tends to be considerably smaller (meaning the gearing is lower) than that on a bike set up for racing, because flatland riders don't need to attain high speeds.

// PARK

Skate parks themselves dictate the styles developed and showcased by the riders using them. Concrete parks with bowls and pools have to be navigated in a certain way, just as wooden parks tend to have ramps and jumps and are generally more challenging, allowing riders to find flowing paths around the park and be a little more creative.

// STREET

There's a clue in the name: street riders practice their discipline in the street using benches, ledges, steps, railings, other street furniture and architectural features as both obstacles to overcome and creative inspiration for tricks. Street riders tend to have no brakes and many opt for a front and back peg on just one side of the bike. Different riders set up their bikes according to their own preferences and personal riding styles.

// TRAILS/DIRT JUMPING

Trails riders ride over sequences of jumps built from compacted earth. Each jump consists of a take off, called a lip, and a landing, with each usually built as separate mounds divided by a gap. This gap can range from 60 cm to over 6 metres (2 to 20 feet) – 3.7 metres (12 feet) seems to be about average. Trails riders focus on flowing smoothly from one jump to the next and performing stylish tricks, while dirt jumpers are interested in jumping higher and performing the craziest possible tricks over larger, less flowing jumps. Trails riders usually run a rear brake and tend to use a gyro to make it easier to do bar spins while airborn. As a general rule, trails/dirt jumping bikes have longer wheelbases and chainstays than other BMX bikes to aid with stability.

// VERT

Vert riding is performed in a half pipe, typically around 2.5 to 3.5 metres (10 to 15 feet) high. Both faces of the ramp have a vertical extension to the transition, hence the name. Riders travel from one side of the ramp to the other, becoming airborn at the top of each side and performing tricks in mid air, such as spins and flips. The biggest ramp ever used in competition is the X Games Big Air Ramp. At 8.2 metres (27 feet) high, it is not for the faint-hearted. Vert riding pioneer and living BMX legend Matt Hoffman has broken bones 50 times, received 200 stitches, suffered from concussion 50 times, had 16 operations and even been in a coma – all as a result of pushing the boundaries of what is possible on a BMX bike.

COMPONENTS

01: FRAME
02: BRAKE LEVERS
03: STEM
04: GYRO ROTOR
05: HEADSET
06: FORKS
07: PEGS
08: HUBS
09: SPROCKET/SPIDER/CHAINRING
10: CHAIN
11: BOTTOM BRACKET
12: CRANKS
13: PEDALS
14: FREEWHEEL/CASSETTE
15: BRAKES
16: BRAKE PADS
17: NIPPLES
18: SPOKES
19: RIMS
20: TYRES
21: BRAKE CABLE
22: SEAT POST CLAMP
23: SEAT POST
24: SEAT
25: GRIPS
26: HANDLEBARS

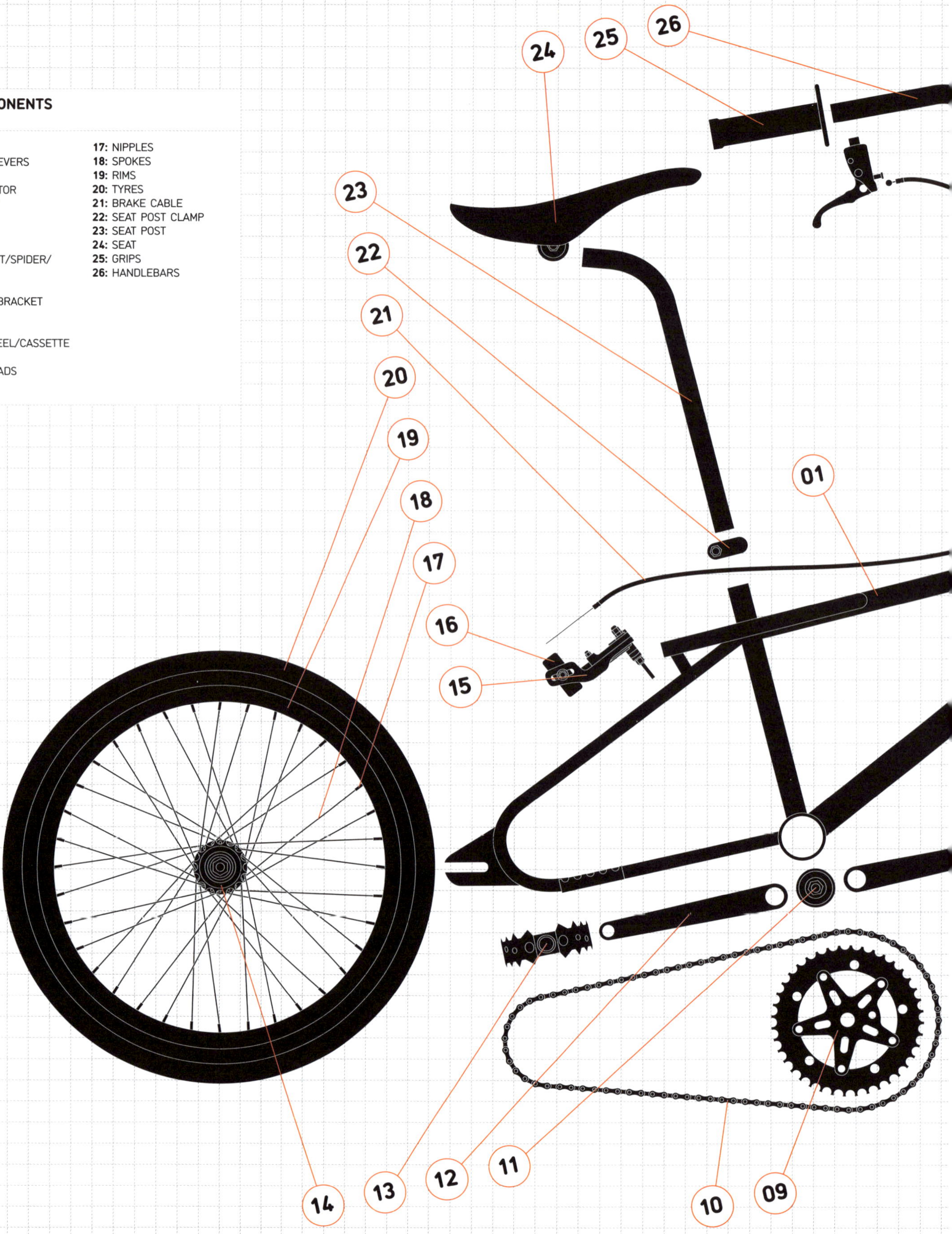

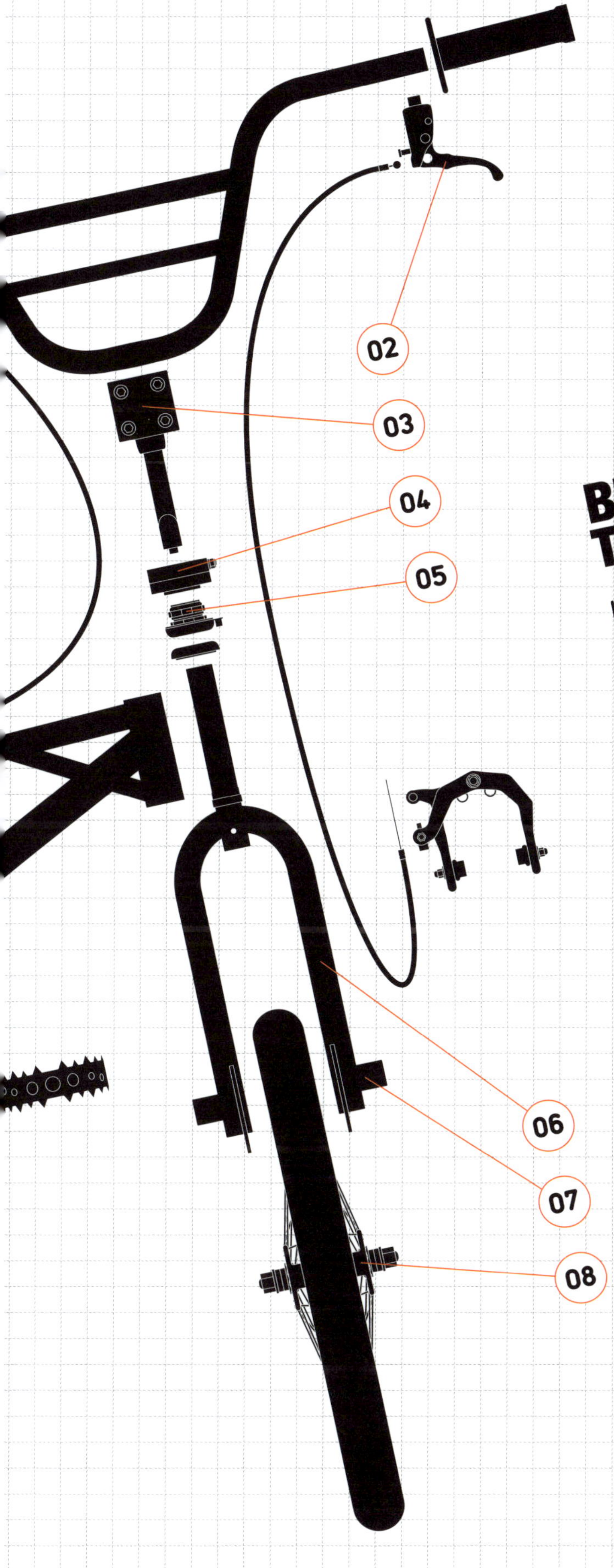

BMX PARTS AND TERMINOLOGY

IN THIS BOOK WE SHOWCASE SOME OF THE BEST BMX BIKES OF ALL TIME AND, WHERE RELEVANT, WE LIST THE COMPONENT PARTS THAT MAKE UP EACH OF THESE BIKES. WE HAVE ALSO CREATED THIS EXPLODED DIAGRAM TO SHOW THE COMPONENTS, BOTH IN TERMS OF WHAT THEY LOOK LIKE AND WHERE THEY FIT ON A BMX.

1970s

1970s

The 1970s was the decade in which BMX was born and it all started on dirt tracks in California. Although Ron Mackler was encouraging kids in his area to race their Schwinn Sting Rays on his dirt track at Palms Park in Santa Monica as early as 1969, it was the promotional and organizational skills of another teenage motocross rider, Scot Breithaupt, that sparked the emergence of the sport we know as BMX today.

Breithaupt, a motocross racer and test rider for Yamaha motorcycles at just 13 years old, set up a track on a disused plot at Seventh and Bellflower in Long Beach, California, in 1970. He tested motorcycles there, but kids used to follow him round the course on their pedal bikes. So he started to encourage local kids, mainly pre-teens, to come and race on their bikes on the track. The word spread fast about these 'pedal-cross' races. One Saturday he had 35 kids racing; the next Saturday 150 turned up. Rather than allow himself to be overwhelmed, Breithaupt's natural ability as a promoter and businessman soon became apparent. He obtained a lease to use the land, insurance, and set up the Bicycle United Motocross Society (B.U.M.S. for short), which acted as a kind of sanctioning body for the emerging sport. It provided rules, a points system, a skill-level structure, racing season and even trophies to be awarded to race winners.

Other sanctioning bodies for the sport would emerge later in the decade as BMX took hold across the United States. Ex-Hollywood stuntman and professional motocross race promoter Ernie Alexander set up the National Bicycle Association (NBA) in 1972. Neither Breithaupt's nor Alexander's sanctioning bodies lasted all that long for one reason or another, but The National Bicycle League (NBL), set up in 1974 by Florida-based George Esser, whose son Greg Esser was one of BMX's first professionals, still exists today. In 1997 it joined USA Cycling, which is part of the *Union Cycliste Internationale* (UCI). Also still going strong today is the American Bicycle Association (ABA), which was created in 1977 by Gene Roden and Merl Mennenga in Chandler, Arizona.

The activities of Breithaupt and others like him on Californian dirt tracks in the very early 1970s got a big boost in 1971 thanks to the opening sequence of motocross documentary *On Any Sunday*. The film was shown in cinemas across the United States and, although it focused entirely on motorcycle racing, the opening sequence showed kids racing customized Schwinns and hand-built bikes around a dirt track and pulling wheelies down suburban streets. Suddenly every kid in the United States wanted to ride a bike like it was a motorcycle.

Meanwhile, on the dirt tracks of California, boys were grouping together into teams, often organized by local bike shops, and finding out (the hard way) that BMX racing put strains on bikes that most of the non-specialist bikes at the time could not withstand. Tubing snapped, bladed forks bent and welds failed, causing bikes to simply crumple under their riders mid race. They just weren't built to be raced off road and land numerous jumps. Bike technology had to develop fast. Fathers of kids involved who were welders or manufacturers started customizing bikes by adding gussets and experimenting with better welding.

Motorcycle manufacturers also saw the potential in BMX and so began making specialist parts and getting involved with BMX racing teams such as Rick Twomey's Rick's Bike Shop team and Scot Breithaupt's team, named after his promotional company, Scot Enterprises (SE for short). Manufacturer Redline (then called Red Line) had considerable input from Twomey in creating the first tubular chromoly fork for BMX bikes in 1974, meaning heavy, bladed forks would soon be a thing of the past. The company also released its first frame in November of that year, known as the '75 Squareback (see page 25). When Redline's bike product tester, a 15 year old named Byron Friday, kept busting single clamp stems (such as the one shown on the 1975 Looptail on page 23), Redline developed a dual-clamp chromoly stem. Friday couldn't break it. You can see one of these on the 1975 Monoshock on page 21. You can also see in this bike the kind of experiments being made

TUBING SNAPPED, BLADED FORKS BENT AND WELDS FAILED, CAUSING BIKES TO SIMPLY CRUMPLE UNDER THEIR RIDERS MID RACE. BIKE TECHNOLOGY HAD TO DEVELOP FAST.

in the mid 1970s with frame builds. However, as this chapter progresses, a more standardized-looking bike emerges. By 1975 the 20-inch wheel had become the standard size for BMX bikes, and chromoly (a high-carbon super-strong and super-light steel alloy containing chromium and molybdenum), was fast becoming the material of choice for BMX frames and forks. Plenty of new manufacturers were founded at this time: Webco, Mongoose, JMC, FMF, DG, Two Wheeler and SE Racing. Stars of the sport also emerged, race winners whose names are now synonymous with the early days of BMX: Stu Thomsen, Harry Leary, Jeff Utterback and Scot Breithaupt himself, a BMX rider who took some beating.

Breithaupt was a few years older than the kids he was encouraging to race and in 1978 he persuaded the various sanctioning bodies (NBA, ABA and NBL) to introduce a cruiser class in which older or bigger kids could race slightly bigger bikes with 26-inch wheels. See page 37 for an example of a cruiser designed by Breithaupt and manufactured through his SE Racing company.

In 1974 the concept of touring took off with Shimano's BMX Tour, which was designed to promote BMX with their team riders acting as ambassadors, endorsing and selling BMX to the masses. In the same year the sport's first magazine emerged, *Bicycle Motocross News*, started and edited by Elaine Holt. Holt is widely credited with having coined the term 'bicycle motocross' and therefore also BMX. Having its own magazine was crucial for the development of BMX in the 1970s. A couple of years later photographer Bob Osborn and daughter Windy would start their own magazine, *Bicycle Motocross Action* (later *BMX Action*). 1974 was also the year of the Yamaha Gold Cup, which was the BMX Championship of California State. It was a BMX competition raced on a portable track (designed by Breithaupt) with finals staged at the LA Coliseum, an NFL football stadium.

As well as racing on reasonably flat tracks, various other disciplines of riding started to emerge throughout the 1970s. There were some killer downhill race courses, such as the one at Soledad Sands in Acton, California, where kids could race from the top of a steep hill to the bottom. For a few years sidehack BMX racing saw bikes fitted with sidecars for a teammate to ride in. The restored 1977 Gary Littlejohn Sidehack on page 28 shows what this type of bike looked like.

Beyond racing, kids started finding new places to have fun on their bikes. Once skateboarders started riding in empty bowl-shaped pools in Beverly Hills, it didn't take long for someone to start ripping them on a bike. Park riding was born. Once riders were airborn on the verts of skate parks and abandoned swimming pool bowls, performing tricks was a natural progression. Fuelled by the kind of photography taken by the likes of Bob and Windy Osborn for *BMX Action* magazine, by the end of the 1970s BMX riders had a new goal beyond mere speed. The question was no longer simply how fast, but how stylishly.

mongoose

BiCYCLE MOTOCROSS NEWS
VOLUME 2 NUMBER 5 Westword Publications, Orange, California JUNE 1975 FIFTY CENTS
SPECIAL ANNIVERSARY ISSUE

Anatomy of a Winner.
Kawasaki
Kawasaki BX200 Motocross Bicycle

COLOR: Charcoal Black
MX OXFORD MOTOR CROSS
• Reinforced welded frame
• Motor Cross saddle and frame cover guard
• Cross bar handle bars with black forged stem
• Cushion shock support
• 20" x 2.125 oversized wheels with heavy duty 120 guage spokes
• 36 Hole Wheel and Track Tires
• Motorcycle quality type heavy duty fork
• Sports action mud guard
• Kick Stand
• Approved BMA-6 reflectors on front and rear wheels, on handle bars and back seat.
Oxford
INTERNATIONAL CORPORATION
P.O. BOX 306
HIGHLAND PARK, ILL. 60035

"WE MAKE IT HAPPEN"
SE RACING
FACTORY ACE STU THOMSEN AND THE "STR-1"

SE RACING AWARDS BANQUET
JANUARY 10th, 1978 – 3p.m.
COME TO "OLD MAN" BREITHAUPT'S HOUSE
3215 E. OCEAN BLVD. LONG BEACH
R.S.V.P. (213) 434-2977

CALIFORNIA STATE CHAMPIONSHIPS
BICYCLE
WHERE TO BOOGIE IN ARIZONA
PLANNING A TRACK
BIG TEST OF THE R&R CR-1
TINKER JUAREZ

ongoose
COMPETITION BICYCLE

FLYIN' OKIE

JAG
BMX
MOTOCROSS BIKES
& ACCESSORY
CATALOG
THE GOLDEN BOOGIE TRACK LEADS TO THE JAMMIN' JAGS!
BOOGIE WITH THE BEST.
MANUFACTURED BY:
B.M.X. PRODUCTS, INC.
9521 IRONDALE AVE., CHATSWORTH, CA 91311
(213) 341-5455
TELEX NO. 69-1310

ROD "BRONCO" BECKERING
"TWO TIMER" STUART THOMSEN
PERRY "THE RIPPER" KRAMER
"The Factory Boys"
SE RACING
BMX INNOVATIONS
1667 East 28th Street, Signal Hill, California 90806

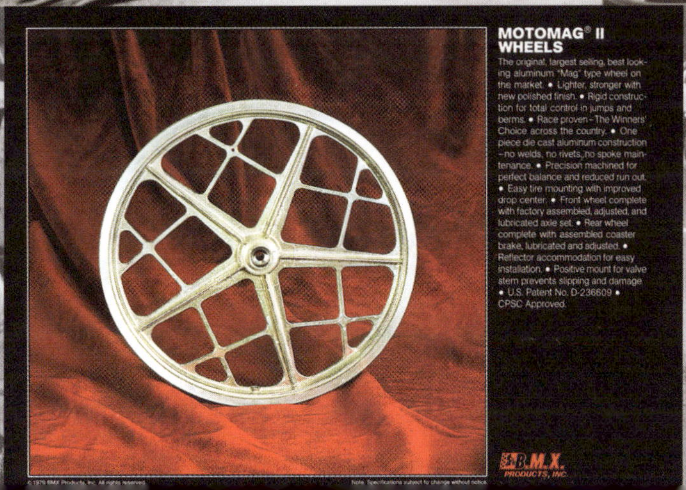
MOTOMAG® II WHEELS
The original, largest selling, best looking aluminum "Mag" type wheel on the market. • Lighter, stronger with new polished finish. • Rigid construction for total control in jumps and berms. • Race proven – The Winners' Choice across the country. • One piece die cast aluminum construction – no welds, no rivets, no spoke maintenance. • Precision machined for perfect balance and reduced run out. • Easy tire mounting with improved drop center. • Front wheel complete with factory assembled, adjusted, and lubricated axle set. • Rear wheel complete with assembled coaster brake, lubricated and adjusted. • Reflector accommodation for easy installation. • Positive mount for valve stem prevents slipping and damage. • U.S. Patent No. D-236609 • CPSC Approved.
B.M.X. PRODUCTS, INC.
© 1979 BMX Products, Inc. All rights reserved.
Note: Specifications subject to change without notice.

1975
KAWASAKI BX200

SUBMITTED BY **MICHAEL DE WIT**

As kids began converting their Schwinn Sting Rays to look like motocross bikes, it made perfect sense that the first production bikes should come from the very same companies that were building those motocross bikes. Yamaha, Suzuki and Kawasaki were all early players in the BMX game and even developed their own race teams. Kawasaki had its fair share of top riders, including the sport's first star, BX200-riding Dave Clinton. The first racer to win an official number one plate of any kind, Clinton was National and American Bicycle Association (NBA) number one when the title was introduced in 1975.

The Kawasaki BX200 featured an aluminium frame with a motorcycle swing-arm design for 'optimim handling and durability'. The rear end also featured two-way adjustable shock absorbers. The bike came with an integrated stem and motorcycle-type steering head, cross-braced handlebars, waffle grips, forged steel one-piece cranks, 'self-cleaning' pedals, MX-style banana seat and a coaster brake. Although the black rubber boot on the forks gives the appearance of suspension, the front forks are in fact rigid.

The bike shown here is almost completely original except for the grips, a survivor of 35 years and counting. 'This bike came along when a great friend of mine (Ezra Fee, R.I.P.) gave me his old BX200 frame that he used to ride as a kid,' explains Vans art director Michael de Wit. 'When looking for parts online, I came across this complete bike for a great price. I'm now waiting anxiously to find the right time for a restoration – there are a few restored ones out there, but not many are as original as this.'

1975
REDLINE MONOSHOCK

SUBMITTED BY **JUAN MATTOS**

Redline began life in 1970 (then called Red Line), as a company of six, making motorcycle frames and parts. It wasn't until 1974 that its first BMX product hit the market in the form of a pair of revolutionary chromoly tubular forks – the first created for push bikes to replace bladed forks. Only a few years later, Redline would have one of the best reputations in BMX, both for its products and for its race team, which boasted one of the sport's early stars, Stompin' Stu Thomsen.

Redline's 1975 Monoshock frame did its best to appeal to motocross fans. In 1974 and 1975 several manufacturers, including Dan Gurney (DG), Yamaha and Webco, also produced frames that incorporated a single 'mono' shock absorber. However, sprung suspension didn't last long as a BMX frame feature. It tended to add weight and dissipate rider energy more than it aided rider comfort.

1975 COOK BROS. 'S' BAR

SUBMITTED BY **JUAN MATTOS**

The Cook Bros. company was set up by two brothers, Craig and Gary Cook, in the mid 1970s. This particular bike was rider Denny Davidow's original race bike and you'd be hard-pressed to find an earlier example of a Cook Bros. bike. Davidow raced from 1975 through to the mid 1980s, originally for Delta Racing Products (DRP) and then for Skyway as their top pro rider for several years.

1975

REDLINE 'PALFREYMAN' LOOPTAIL

SUBMITTED BY **JUAN MATTOS**

Named after John 'Snaggletooth' Palfreyman – an early pioneer of the sport who rode with Rick's Bike Shop team in the early days of BMX racing, along with fellow teammates David Clinton, Doug Takahashi and Thom Lund. Palfreyman was certainly among the top five ranking riders in 1974–75 along with David Clinton, Bobby Encinas, John George and Stu Thomsen.

According to its owner, Juan Mattos, this is the first rigid frame manufactured by Redline and is the first of only two ever produced. It was Best of Show winner at Rockford in 2004.

1975
JMC XP-2

SUBMITTED BY **JUAN MATTOS**

Jim Melton Cyclery (JMC) started as a bike shop in 1969 and sponsored BMX riders in the 1970s, including Harry Leary, Clint Miller, David 'Tinker' Juarez and Darrell Young. While JMC began manufacturing BMX bikes in 1977, this bike, also known as the JMC Experimental 2, predates JMC's first production run of BMX bikes and was built as rider Harry Leary's personal team bike. XP-2 is the frame serial number of this particular bike.

1976
REDLINE SQUAREBACK

SUBMITTED BY **JUAN MATTOS**

Redline launched its very first production BMX frame in late 1974, with no small amount of design input from Rick Twomey and his Rick's Bike Shop race team. The frame was to be known as the '75 Squareback on account of its angled rear stays with rectangular tubing. Shown here is the '76 Squareback. It sports a larger gusset than the previous model, which had a small gusset like the one on the Palfreyman Looptail on page 23.

The rear stays on the '76 Squareback are still made of rectangular chromoly tubing, but are smoother in the bends than those of its predecessor.

1976
TWO WHEELER STROKER II

SUBMITTED BY **JUAN MATTOS**

In the mid 1970s Two Wheeler had great riders riding for them, such as Jeff Bottema, Tinker Juarez and Brian Lewis. Lewis became the first cover boy for *Bicycle Motocross Action*, appearing on a Stroker II on the cover of the magazine's debut issue in late 1976.

Founded and owned by Marshal Wheeler, Two Wheeler's Stroker frames were a huge success on BMX race tracks in the mid 1970s and are still popular with collectors now – no doubt for their distinctive square-framed tubing and their place in BMX history.

1977

ROGER DECOSTER (SHORT)

SUBMITTED BY **GLYNN HICKS**

FRAME: ROGER DECOSTER SHORT
FORKS: ROGER DECOSTER
BARS: MONGOOSE STAINLESS
STEM: TUF-NECK
HEADSET: TANGE AW-27
CRANKS: ASHTABULA 165MM
SPROCKET: THREE ARROWS
PEDALS: KKT
CHAIN: IZUMI
HUBS: ACS DATED 1977
RIMS: ARAYA 7B (THICK SPOKES)
TYRES: NOBBIES
SEAT: KASHIMAX
SEAT POST: FLUTED ALLOY
SEAT POST CLAMP: TUF-NECK
GRIPS: WINNER'S CIRCLE

Roger DeCoster was a motocross rider who won five World Championships racing 500cc bikes. He was widely recognized as one of the best riders of his time.

During the 1970s it was clear marketing sense for BMX manufacturers to team up with big-name riders and launch products off the back of this relationship. The Roger DeCoster brand was set up by BMX Products to be sold directly to Schwinn.

Made in the United States from 4130 chromoly, these frames, which were available in a short or a long version (both with the distinctive oval-shaped gusset perforation), are a modern-day collector's item.

Glynn Hicks, ex-Australian-BMX champion, found a DeCoster Short on eBay in Canada. He says, 'Postage was going to be $300 to Australia, and it just so happened that I was heading over to Whistler to mountain bike with a buddy for our 40th birthdays. The seller dropped it off at a bike shop in Vancouver for me to pick up in person.

'We must have caught two trains, a bus and walked a couple of Ks, taking over an hour and half to get there, only to realize that there were three bike shops with the same name. We were heading for the wrong one!

'Eventually, when we found the correct shop, it made it all worthwhile as I first caught sight of the frame. It wasn't just a regular DeCoster, but a rare shorty! I assembled this one as a rider with some classic parts like the Araya 7B heavy-duty wheelset and Tuf-Neck stem.'

1977

GARY LITTLEJOHN SIDEHACK

SUBMITTED BY **ANDREAS STEVENS**

As motocross was such a huge influence on the development of the sport of BMX, sidehack racing was a natural progression for those kids already riding modified Sting Rays. Sidehacks were pioneered in the early 1970s by John Palfreyman and Doug Takahashi, who were later sponsored by Rick Twomey and his Rick's Bike Shop team. Raced on downhill dirt tracks, sidehacks eventually faded into obscurity in the early 1980s.

The Gary Littlejohn shown here was lovingly restored by DJ and producer Andreas Stevens, who purchased it from its original owner. 'They had raced it until the early 1980s and then put it away and kept it until 2005, which is when I bought it and fully restored it to the way you see it now.'

Gary Littlejohn was originally a manufacturer of motorcycle frames and gas tanks, as well as being a part-time Hollywood stuntman.

FRAME: GARY LITTLEJOHN
FORKS: TANGE 500
BARS: RACE INC.
STEM: SUGINO
HEADSET: TANGE
CRANKS: ASHTABULA
SPROCKET: SUGINO THREE ARROWS
PEDALS: KKT RAT TRAPS
CHAIN: HKK SMOKER
WHEELS: MONGOOSE MOTOMAG 2
TYRES: CHENG SHIN
SEAT: SCHWINN BANANA
SEAT POST: SCHWINN
SEAT POST CLAMP: ADDICKS
GRIPS: OURY

1977

FMF TEAM BIKE

SUBMITTED BY **JUAN MATTOS**

Like DG Racing (see opposite), Flying Machine Factory (FMF) started out as a motocross accessory manufacturer and became involved in BMX frame building and sponsorship of top riders. FMF disappeared from the world of BMX in the early 1980s, but reappeared in 2002 and continues to make high-end BMX racing bikes, components and accessories today.

This is a 1977 Team Replica Bike and, according to its owner, collector Juan Mattos, is the only mint example known to exist.

1977
DG-1

SUBMITTED BY **JUAN MATTOS**

DG Racing began life as a motorcycle parts company and was named after the company's two founders, Dan and Gary. Gary's son Kevin rode MX and BMX, and so DG got involved in BMX in 1975. They soon hired Chuck Robinson (who was later to form his own BMX manufacturing company, Robinson Racing) to run its race team. Robinson selected some of the best riders of the time to race for DG, including Jeff Bottema and Stu Thomsen. This particular bike, owned by collector Juan Mattos, used to belong to Jeff Bottema and is in absolute original condition, complete with a set of super-rare dual-colour Oakley 1 grips.

1978
WEBCO REPLICA

SUBMITTED BY **ANDREAS STEVENS**

FRAME: WEBCO REPLICA
FORKS: COOK BROS.
BARS: REDLINE V
STEM: ROUGH RIDER
HEADSET: TANGE
CRANKS: CAMPAGNOLO STRADA
SPROCKET: CAMPAGNOLO
PEDALS: KKT RAT TRAPS
CHAIN: SEDIS
RIMS: ARAYA 7B
HUBS: CAMPY LOW FLANGE
TYRES: CHENG SHIN
SEAT: ELINA SUPER PRO
SEAT POST: FLUTED ALUMINIUM
BRAKE: WEINMANN CENTER PULL
GRIPS: OAKLEY 1

Another motocross company turned bicycle manufacturer, Webco's foray into the world of BMX started with a sponsorship deal with the legendary Rick's Bike Shop team. Rick Twomey (the Rick in Rick's Bike Shop team) had been making and customizing his own frames and components for his team riders until teaming up with Webco in 1973. With Twomey's guidance, Webco produced the very first production triangular BMX frame. The initial Webco bikes, also featuring the first incarnation of Skip Hess' famous Motomag wheels, were unveiled at the 1974 Yamaha Gold Cup Finals in Los Angeles.

The bike shown here is a rare example of a survivor. It belonged to a very well-known racer from southern California who prefers to remain anonymous. All the parts are original; nothing has been replaced or altered.

1978
G-BOY

SUBMITTED BY **JUAN MATTOS**

Not an awful lot is known about G-Boy frames, other than they have probably the largest and most perforated gusset in the history of BMX frame manufacturing. G-Boy frames were produced in limited numbers at a welding shop in Carona, California, from 1976 to 1979, inspired by the frame geometry of a bike by a rival manufacturer: Webco.

This particular 1978 G-Boy, owned by Juan Mattos, sports the only pair of G-Boy prototype forks known to exist at the time of writing.

1978

SE RACING JU-6

SUBMITTED BY **JUAN MATTOS**

The JU-6, Scot Breithaupt's first frame design, was named in honour of SE Racing team rider Jeff Utterback's sixth place national ranking in 1977.

Around ten JU-6 frames are known to exist at the time of writing. Of those, two have round top tubes but the standard version (shown here) features flat-edged, 'floval' top and down tubes designed by Breithaupt to give the bike frame extra rigidity and strength. Only months after the bike had appeared in press adverts, Utterback left SE to join his father's new BMX company, GJS (see page 36). Almost as soon as it had been conceived, the JU-6 was discontinued. Instead the frame design was modified, a gusset was added and the new iteration was named after another SE Racing rider, Perry Kramer. That bike, the PK Ripper (see page 58), is without doubt one of the best-loved and most popular old-school BMX bikes of all time.

1978
REDLINE PROLINE

SUBMITTED BY **GLYNN HICKS**

This bike is a 1978 Redline Proline, belonging to the Australian collector Glynn Hicks. He says, 'I purchased the frame and fork out of California. I built it for my brother and loved it so much that I bought it off him. My brother raced this exact type of bike back in the late 70s so I have built it as close to the original as I can remember by looking back on old photos. I've taken it on a few organized "old school" rides and it rolls as smooth as silk. I'm really happy with this build, definitely a keeper.'

FRAME: REDLINE PROLINE
FORKS: REDLINE PROLINE
BARS: NOS PROLINE V BARS
STEM: REDLINE BRUT
HEADSET: TANGE AW-27
CRANKS: REDLINE 400
SPROCKET: SUGINO
PEDALS: KKT RAT TRAPS
CHAIN: IZUMI
HUBS: TNT REVOLVER
RIMS: NOS ARAYA 7C
TYRES: RAINBOW LABEL TIOGA COMP III
SEAT: KASHIMAX
SEAT POST: RACING
SEAT POST CLAMP: ACS
BRAKE: SHIMANO TOURNEY
LEVER: SHIMANO
GRIPS: A'ME
EXTRAS: REPRO PAD SET

1978
JMC SHORT

SUBMITTED BY **MICHAEL DE WIT**

The first production JMC Short was made in 1977, but this restoration doesn't obsess over recreating an original. Michael de Wit, the bike's owner, explains: 'The frame/fork/bars were given to me by a really good friend a few years ago. Excited to restore it to its original state, I contacted Jim Melton and gave him the serial number to find out what the original colour was, since all the parts I had were in a raw finish. He told me that according to his records it was sold like that in 1978 to a skateshop in Atlanta. This got me thinking I really wanted to restore the bike in more of a retro way, rather then bringing it back to an original set up.'

The new orange colourway was inspired by the national colour of de Wit's birthplace, the Netherlands, and it's the same orange as that used on the Ford 021c concept car that was created by one of de Wit's favourite designers, Marc Newson. Regarding the black components: 'Jim was already producing the black pads and stickers, so it only seemed natural to do the parts in black,' says de Wit. 'I left it brakeless, since I felt it was a way cleaner look and now plenty of riders don't have brakes. The DK sprocket and pedals are a dedication to Colin Winkleman (R.I.P.), who died in 2005, the year I finished the bike.'

1978 JAG BMX CAFE RACER

SUBMITTED BY **GLYNN HICKS**

Formed in 1978, JAG BMX is a company steeped in BMX history. Its current-day president Renny Roker raced, rode and worked for JAG back in the day and helped introduce the sport to a global audience. JAG frames were made by Skip Hess' company, Mongoose.

JAG introduced the first BMX World Championships in 1978, which ran for six years (until 1984).

At the time of writing JAG is planning and building a Global BMX & Excellence Centre, which will contain Olympic-standard race tracks as well as training and fitness facilities to help the sport continue to grow and thrive through rider training.

The bikes on this page are very early JAG products, both from Glynn Hicks' collection. The Café Racer was bought on eBay from a seller in the United States. It was in rough condition and the top of the seat tube had snapped off. It needed a lot of work.

'My motivation for this build was an episode from the classic 70s TV show *CHiPs* which featured the JAG BMXs. I have had the frame powder-coated dark chocolate brown, built with black Z rims, red V-bars and a Carlisle Aggressor front nobbie tyre.'

FRAME: JAG CAFÉ RACER (HALF CHROMOLY)
FORKS: TANGE
BARS: REDLINE V-BAR
STEM: SUNTOUR
HEADSET: TANGE AW-27
CRANKS: ASHTABULA
SPROCKET: THREE ARROWS
PEDALS: KINGSBURY PROD.
CHAIN: IZUMI
HUBS: SUNTOUR
RIMS: ACS Z-RIM
TYRES: CHENG SHIN REAR; CARLISLE AGGRESSOR FRONT
SEAT: LEATHER KASHIMAX
SEAT POST: FLUTED ALLOY
SEAT POST CLAMP: SCHWINN
BRAKE: DIA-COMPE
LEVER: SHIMANO
GRIPS: A'ME

1979 JAG BMX TEAM

SUBMITTED BY **GLYNN HICKS**

FRAME: JAG TEAM
FORKS: ROGER DECOSTER
BARS: ALLOY RACE INC.
STEM: MONGOOSE
HEADSET: TANGE AW-27
CRANKS: SHIMANO DURA-ACE
SPROCKET: SHIMANO 43T
PEDALS: UNION
CHAIN: IZUMI
HUBS: SHIMANO
RIMS: ARAYA 7C
TYRES: SNAKE BELLY COPIES
SEAT: SUEDE KASHIMAX
SEAT POST: FLUTED
SEAT POST CLAMP: MONGOOSE
BRAKE: TOURNEY
LEVER: SHIMANO PRE-BENT (CHARLIE GNARLEY)
GRIPS: A'ME
EXTRAS: JAG PAD SET

FRAME: GJS A-FRAME
FORKS: RACE INC.
BARS: REDLINE PROLINE V-BAR
STEM: TUF-NECK
HEADSET: TANGE MX-2
CRANKS: SUGINO 175
SPROCKET: PHIL WOOD SPIDER, SHIMANO 44T CHAINRING, SUNTOUR CHAINRING BOLTS
PEDALS: KKT RAT TRAPS
CHAIN: HKK SMOKER
HUBS: SHIMANO LARGE-FLANGE
RIMS: ARAYA 7C
TYRES: CYCLE PRO BLACKWALL 20 X 2.125 FRONT, CYCLE PRO SNAKE BELLY SKIN WALL 20 X 1.75 REAR
SEAT: CINELLI UNICANITOR #2
SEAT POST: CHROMOLY
SEAT POST CLAMP: SUNTOUR
BRAKE: SHIMANO TOURNEY
LEVER: SHIMANO PRE-BENT
GRIPS: OAKLEY II
EXTRAS: SHIMANO 333 16T FREEWHEEL, UNION SS SPOKES WITH BRASS NIPPLES, SCOTT MATHAUSER BRAKE PADS, SHIMANO BRAKE CABLE AND CABLE CLAMPS, VINYL POWERLITE FRAME AND BAR PADS BY RAD PADS, TUF-NECK STEM PAD, CUSTOM NUMBER PLATE

1979
GJS A-FRAME

SUBMITTED BY **MICHAEL GAMSTETTER**

GJS was set up in 1977 by George Utterback, father of SE team rider Jeff Utterback. George was a welder–fabricator and had raced drag motorcycles in the 1960s. The letters GJS stand for George, Jeff and Scott (Jeff's brother). The emergence of the company meant that Jeff left the SE Racing team to join the family business only months after SE's Scot Breithaupt had created SE's first signature frame for him, named the JU-6 (see page 32).

The A-Frame was GJS' first BMX frame and it broke the mould. It was the first ever frame to incorporate tubes for gusset support instead of sheet metal. The first generation of A-Frames were available in red, orange, yellow, blue or black. In late 1979 the yellow and orange colour options were dropped and a chrome option added to the line. The frame underwent various tweaks during production between 1977 and 1985 and only a few more than 3,000 frames were made. Around 1980 GJS started to make and sell forks, bars and also a seat post clamp. In 1983 GJS designed a freestyle frame. The very first one, restored beautifully by collector Juan Mattos, is on page 69.

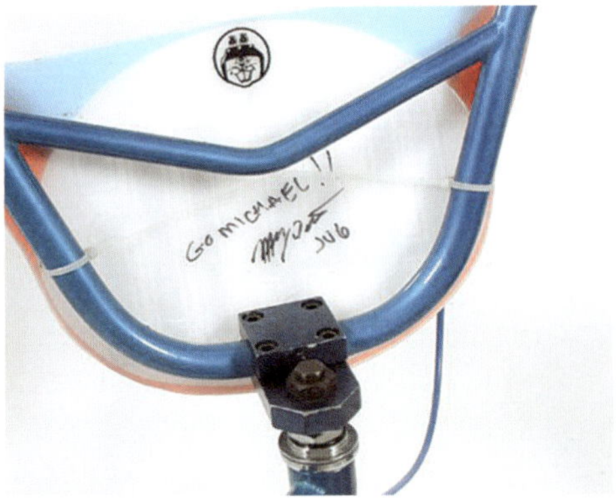

1979
SE RACING OM FLYER

SUBMITTED BY **JUAN MATTOS**

In the late 1970s SE Racing's Scot Breithaupt – already dubbed the Old Man (OM) of BMX because he was a little older than many of the riders and had achieved so much in terms of promoting the sport and organizing events – was keen for taller kids and adults to still keep riding and competing even if they had outgrown the 20-inch wheel bikes they had started out on. In 1978 Breithaupt persuaded the various sanctioning bodies of BMX at the time (NBA, ABA and NBL) to incorporate larger wheel (26-inch) bikes in new cruiser classes, thus attracting more adults to BMX.

It was on an OM Flyer that Breithaupt, the bike's designer, set a long-distance jump record – aided by a downhill run that helped him reach a speed 50–60 miles (80–90 kilometres) per hour – of 23 metres (76 feet), the average length of three jumps. That record stood for ten years. It was landing those jumps, after several seconds of being airborn, that gave Breithaupt a name for his company's new forks: Landing Gear. The forks have been among BMX's most popular products of all time.

From Miami-based collector Juan Mattos' BMX collection, this SE Racing OM Flyer of circa 1979 is, in fact, the very one that the OM himself rode in competition for many years. SE never produced chrome-finished OM Flyers commercially, this was produced specially for Breithaupt, custom-made with double-butted tubes and mitred joints.

1980s

swatch
swatch
swatch
swatch

1980s

Ask any BMX rider about the 1980s and the first word you'll hear is 'freestyle'. In other words, riding not to win a race, but to showcase creativity on a BMX bike.

Towards the latter half of the 1970s, riders like Stu Thomsen and John Palfreyman were already known for park riding and ripping swimming pools, such as the infamous Keyhole in Beverly Hills. But in April 1980, Mongoose team rider David 'Tinker' Juarez appeared on the cover of *BMX Action* magazine (vol. 5, issue 4), shown airborn above a skate park, along with the accolade 'King of the Skateparks'. Inside the magazine was a picture-led feature showing Juarez performing vertical freestyle tricks at Lakewood skate park in Lakewood, California. He was airborn in almost every shot.

Meanwhile, at the offices of *BMX Action*, its resident cartoonist – a young rider called Bob Haro – had formed the very first BMX trick team with R.L. Osborn (son of *BMX Action* head honcho, Bob Osborn). The duo regularly tested bikes for review in the magazine and Haro devised and perfected countless tricks, many of which he revealed in special how-to features in the magazine. The pair first performed as the BMX Action Trick Team at the 1978 Winternationals in Chandler, Arizona, organized by the ABA. However, it was in 1981 that Haro, this time with Bob Morales, travelled on tour showing off tricks all over the Midwest, the East and parts of Canada to crowds of people that had never seen anything like it. The same year, Haro was a stunt rider in a film being directed by Steven Spielberg. That film, *E.T.: The Extra-Terrestrial* (often referred to as just *E.T.*), catapulted BMX on to cinema screens, just as *On Any Sunday* had done ten years earlier. Only *E.T.* got a much wider audience than the 1970s motocross documentary. It was a huge, international box office smash. BMX just went global.

In the early 1980s Bob Haro became a well-known name in BMX for his BMX illustrations, his small business (Haro Designs) selling race number plates, and his how-to trick riding features in *BMX Action*. Gradually his name was becoming synonymous with trick riding and freestyle. In 1981 he approached Steve Johnson at Torker to manufacture the first specifically-for-freestyle BMX bike frame, the Haro Freestyler.

Produced in shiny chrome, the Haro Freestyler incorporated Torker's signature double top tube design, which makes it easier to balance when standing on the frame. The frame also sported a thicker headtube than the Torker race bikes of the time, a hefty gusset between the down tube and the chunky one-and-a-quarter-inch headtube. Other differences between the Haro Freestyler and Torker's race bikes included thicker rear dropouts to handle tricks in which the rear end of the bike is whipped round, a steeper steering-tube angle (for sharper steering) and a steeper seat-tube angle. The frame had built-in slotted coaster brake brackets. The fork dropouts were hefty and the Haro Freestyler frame, as with most Torker-built frames of the time, were heat-treated to give them even more strength.

Freestyle had a founding father and now its own dedicated bike. Haro's new company, Haro Bikes, supported and sponsored talented freestyle riders, including Bob Morales, Eddie Fiola, Mike Dominguez, Ron Wilkerson, Dennis McCoy, Mat Hoffman and many more. These guys and others like them became the star proponents of freestyle, and other manufacturers such as GT, Skyway and Hutch were quick to start producing dedicated freestyle bikes. Now this new aspect of BMX needed to get organized... It didn't take long. In 1982, after meeting a talented park rider called Eddie Fiola, Haro's trick riding buddy Bob Morales founded the Amateur Skate Park Association (ASPA) to organize BMX freestyle events. By 1984, the ASPA had morphed into the American Freestyle Association (AFA), freestyle's first governing body.

Freestyle was then, and is still, about showing off. Let's not make any bones about it. How high can you go? How many tricks can you pull off? As well as specific-to-freestyle geometry, bikes started to sport innovative features to enable new tricks. The rotor, designed by Dale Cooper to enable

STEVEN SPIELBERG'S FILM *E.T.* CATAPULTED BMX ON TO CINEMA SCREENS, LIKE *ON ANY SUNDAY* TEN YEARS EARLIER. ONLY *E.T.* GOT A MUCH WIDER AUDIENCE THAN THE 1970S MOTOCROSS DOCUMENTARY. IT WAS A HUGE, INTERNATIONAL BOX-OFFICE SMASH. BMX JUST WENT GLOBAL.

In the early 1980s Bob Haro became well-know for his BMX illustrations, producing cartoons for both *BMX Weekly* magazine and *BMX Action*.

tangle-free brakes, appeared in 1985. If you had a rotor and also ran your front brake cable through a hollow bolt stem and out through the fork, it meant you could spin your bars as much as you wanted without having to spin them back to disentangle the brake cables. Axle extenders or pegs also started to appear in the mid 1980s, which enabled all sorts of new tricks.

In 1984, Bob Osborn of *BMX Action* fame started a new sister publication called *Freestylin'*, dedicated to all things freestyle. Unofficial, unsponsored freestyle teams started to pop up, such as the Curb Dogs of San Francisco or The Gork Trick Team. These were full of amateurs, kids who weren't affiliated to a specific manufacturer and didn't have logo-covered uniforms to wear, but put just as much time as the pros into learning and perfecting their craft. Using the name of his former trick team, 2-Hip, pro freestyler Ron Wilkerson started organizing and promoting sponsor-free, initially low-key events for fellow riders. These events weren't about promoting manufacturers wares, but about riders getting together and pushing the limits of what they could achieve. The first of many 2-Hip King of Vert (KOV) events took place in Le Sueur, Minnesota, in November 1986.

Towards the end of the 1980s, after the best part of two decades of non-stop growth, the popularity of BMX began to waver. Sales plummeted, businesses went under and all the professional riders of the late 1970s and the pioneers of freestyle in the early 1980s were growing up. Some even said that BMX was dead. But, as we know now, BMX was far from dead and buried. A new generation of riders were coming through who spent most of their time riding in the streets or practising in car parks and their back yards, just like skateboarders were doing. Riders like Kevin Jones from Pennsylvania were inventing never-dreamed-of tricks in the late 1980s that would give birth to present-day flatland riding. Around the same time, a young freestyle rider by the name of Mat Hoffman was coming into his own. Hoffman made not just a name for himself, but also brought BMX to an even wider audience by covering new ground and taking BMX to dizzying new heights. Literally.

WILD THING
HARO

up...
up...
and away
Fly the mongoose Kos Kruiser

FIRST PLACE
SKYWAY FREESTYLE TEAM
GET IT TOGETHER WITH SKYWAY!
SKYWAY
WE BUILD 'EM BETTER

KUWAHARA
NOVA...SETTING THE PACE.

BICYCLE MOTOCROSS ACTION
THE WORLD'S LARGEST BMX PUBLICATION
FREE HUGE CONTEST for 8 bicycles and tons of BMX stuff
TINKER JUAREZ: the king of the skateparks
INDY '79 World Championships
More Shoot-Out
HOT TRACK SECTIONS
How to modify your alloy cranks for quick release

FREESTYLIN'
BMX MAGAZINE
SUMMER 1984
FREE WITH THIS MAG: GIANT COLOR POSTER
TRICKS YOU CAN DO:
COMPETITION: KING OF THE SKATEPARKS
FREESTYLIN' IN SAN FRANCISCO

STREET THRASHIN'
RACE BASHIN'
SKYWAY
RECREATION

BMX WEEKLY
VOLUME 3 · ISSUE 6
40p
THE WORLD'S LARGEST FORTNIGHTLY BMX PUBLICATION
GREAT CRUISER COMPARISON
RACING: ASHTON NATIONAL
HUGE PULL-OUT COLOUR POSTER
GO FOR IT!

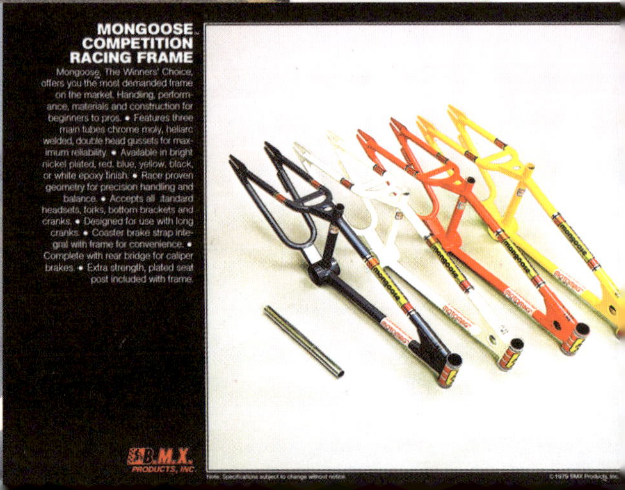
MONGOOSE COMPETITION RACING FRAME
Mongoose, The Winners' Choice, offers you the most demanded frame on the market. Handling, performance, materials and construction for beginners to pros. • Features three main tubes chrome moly, heliarc welded, double head gussets for maximum reliability. • Available in bright nickel plated, red, blue, yellow, black, or white epoxy finish. • Race proven geometry for precision handling and balance. • Accepts all standard headsets, forks, bottom brackets and cranks. • Designed for use with long cranks. • Coaster brake strap integral with frame for convenience. • Complete with rear bridge for caliper brakes. • Extra strength, plated seat post included with frame.
B.M.X. PRODUCTS, INC.

BIKES
MASTER
SPORT
MASTER/SPORT TEAM SERIES
3

SE FREESTYLE
MOVIN' TO THE STREETS
NOT A THROUGH STREET

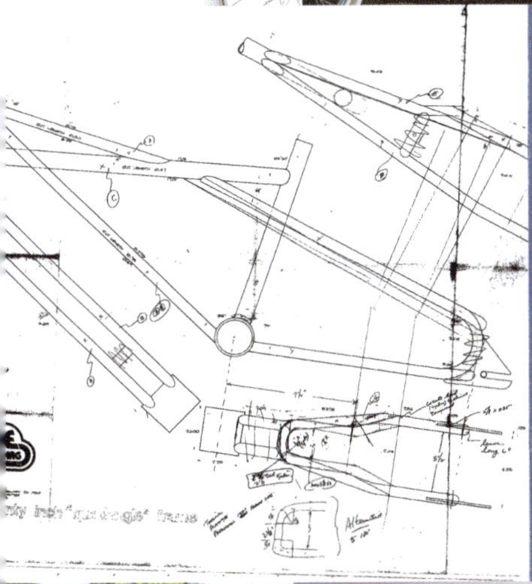

RALEIGH
BURNERS
Go for it with Aero Frame Burners

STAR STRUCK!
HUTCH
HYPERFORMANCE BMX HUTCH

BMX Action Bike
Number 20 July 1984
60p
FREE INSIDE ANDY RUFFELL BMX BOOK
SPECIAL ISSUE
BMX ON TV
(The Inside Story)
WIN THIS BIKE
We give away Bob Morales' GT Performer
Andy Ruffell
Bob Haro Greg Hill
Eddie Fiola Tim March

THE ULTIMATE PROFILE
TEST
Zagar's pro-style profile
Profile beauty is definitely more than skin deep. This scoot may look like a full-on show bike, but one lap around a track and you realize that the bike means business.
"We'd rather be known as the Cadillac of the industry. We're not interested in building 10,000 bikes a year, just producing the absolute best we possibly can." That's Jim Alley, proud owner of Profile Racing, Inc. talking. One look at any one of his fine line of BMX framesets or components and you'll realize that he knows exactly what he's talking about. And exactly what it takes to build the best BMX has to offer. Jim Alley and Profile Racing's "multi-million-dollar machine shop" located in St.
one for our readers. Just for pure entertainment, of course. If you think that we would build a dream machine for the editorial staff around here, you're wrong. What would we possibly do with a bike like this? A fully race-ready weapon that's ready to seek and destroy any and all comers? A bike that would turn the head of even the most equipment-conscious pro? A bike that attracts BMX groupies like nothing we've seen before? Seriously, what for? For the nonstop fun of it!
ERIC RUPE, RICHARD ZAGARS AND
PROFILE'S BEST SHOT
When you check the specs, you'll notice that Profile almost manufactures a complete BMX bike: frame, fork, bars, seatpost, crankset, bottom bracket, stem hubs and pedals. With the exception of the new and improved pedals, which weren't ready at press time, we received everything, plus a CARE package of choice Japanese components, to build up the bike.
If there's one thing that rings true when you look over any one piece of Profile equip, it has to be quality. This

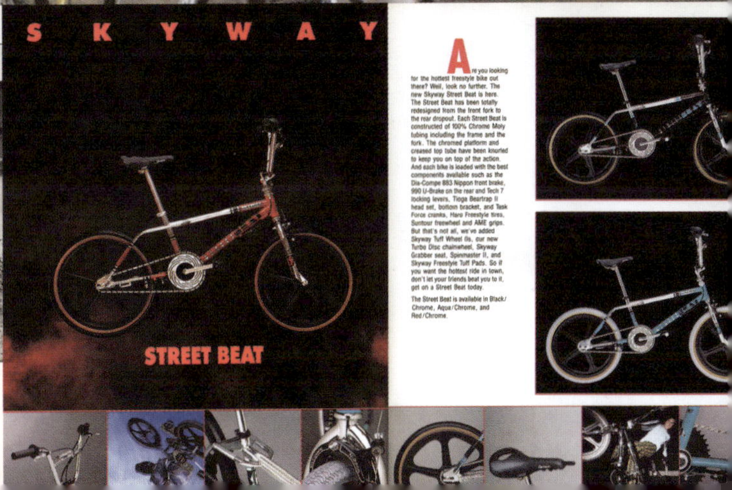
SKYWAY
STREET BEAT
Are you looking for the hottest freestyle bike out there? Well, look no further. The new Skyway Street Beat is here. The Street Beat has been totally redesigned from the front fork to the rear dropout. Each Street Beat is constructed of 100% Chrome Moly tubing including the frame and the fork. The chromed platform and creased top tube have been knurled to keep you on top of the action. And each bike is loaded with the best components available such as the Dia-Compe 883 Nippon front brake, 990 U-Brake on the rear and Tech 7 locking levers, Tioga Beartrap II head set, bottom bracket, and Task Force cranks, Haro Freestyle tires, Suntour freewheel and AME grips. But that's not all, we've added Skyway Tuff Wheel IIs, our new Turbo Disc chainwheel, Skyway Grabber seat, Spinmaster II, and Skyway Freestyle Tuff Pads. So if you want the hottest ride in town, don't let your friends beat you to it, get on a Street Beat today.
The Street Beat is available in Black/Chrome, Aqua/Chrome, and Red/Chrome.

1980
BMX PRODUCTS BLUE MAX

SUBMITTED BY **GLYNN HICKS**

FRAME: BMX PRODUCTS BLUE MAX
FORKS: TANGE
BARS: STAMPED STAINLESS MONGOOSE
STEM: MONGOOSE
HEADSET: TANGE AW-27
CRANKS: STAMPED MONGOOSE
SPROCKET: SHIMANO 43T
PEDALS: UNION
CHAIN: IZUMI
HUBS: SHIMANO HIGH FLANGE
RIMS: ARAYA 7C
TYRES: SNAKE BELLY COPIES
SEAT: BLACK KASHIMAX
SEAT POST: RACE INC.
SEAT POST CLAMP: DIA-COMPE COPY
BRAKE: SHIMANO TOURNEY
LEVER: SHIMANO TOURNEY
GRIPS: MONGOOSE
EXTRAS: CUSTOM BLUE MAX PAD SET

Ex-drag racer Skip Hess formed BMX Products in 1974 and the Motomag 1 wheel was the company's first product. BMX Products went on to manufacture frames for many well-known BMX brands and even created some of its own, including Mongoose, Blue Max and the Roger DeCoster brand, which was sold immediately to Schwinn.

'To my knowledge the Blue Max brand was made to supply the US Army bases throughout the world in the early '80s,' says the owner of this Blue Max, Glynn Hicks.

A friend of his had won the frame on an old-school BMX forum. 'I wangled a trade with him for it,' Hicks tells us. 'This was an easy build as I had most of the parts already and it went together really well, with all Mongoose running gear. I like this bike because it's a bit different. And I don't ride this one, it's just too collectable. It hangs on my wall.'

FRAME: JMC STANDARD LONG
FORKS: JMC
BARS: PROLINE V-BAR
STEM: TUF-NECK
HEADSET: TANGE AW-27
CRANKS: PROFILE BOX
SPROCKET: SUGINO 42T
PEDALS: BLACK HAIR
CHAIN: IZUMI
HUBS: SUNTOUR
RIMS: ARAYA 7B
TYRES: COMP III (BLUE GREY LABEL)
SEAT: ELINA
SEAT POST: FLUTED
SEAT POST CLAMP: CUSTOM
BRAKE: SHIMANO TOURNEY
LEVER: SHIMANO DX
GRIPS: OAKLEY .5S
EXTRAS: REPRO BMXA PAD SET

1980 JMC STANDARD LONG

SUBMITTED BY **GLYNN HICKS**

This 1980 Standard Long, from Glynn Hicks' collection, is one he acquired as a frame and fork set from a shop that had closed down in the 1990s. The shop owner had stored it at his home for the past 20 years, after it had been traded in for a new bike in the late 1980s. It was in bad shape, with holes drilled in the top tube for brake cables and, although the paint was original, it needed to be resprayed.

'This is a recent build (2011) and I was excited to score it as I've always wanted one for my collection,' says Hicks. 'It is considered one of the highest quality race frames of its time. The uniqueness of this frame and fork is the oval tubing.'

1981 JMC BLACK SHADOW

SUBMITTED BY **MICHAEL GAMSTETTER**

Originally designed for team rider Kim Jarboe, JMC first introduced the Black Shadow in March 1980. The frame came about after pro racer Denny Davidow told JMC's Jim Melton that Jarboe would be unbeatable if he had a frame with a steeper headtube angle. The Black Shadow went on to become a highly desirable frame, with a lightweight reputation and a black paint finish.

'I finally got the bike I wanted when I was 14,' says its owner, Michael Gamstetter. 'In 1981 I sold my beloved Torker to buy something longer. I had wanted a JMC since 1978. When an area shop started carrying JMC circa 1980, I decided that a JMC would be my next bike. I went in to buy a Black Shadow with a Euro BB, but the shop was out of Shadows and had no forks. The only frame in stock was a blue Long Standard. Being an impatient 14 year old, I took it. I had immediate buyer's remorse, but I loved the bike's ride. Soon I was planning how I would replace it with the Black Shadow frame and forks of my dreams. I never did, until recently.'

FRAME: JMC BLACK SHADOW WITH EURO BB
FORKS: JMC BLACK SHADOW
BARS: PRO NECK ALLOY
STEM: PRO NECK
HEADSET: O.M.A.S. WITH DIRT SKIRT
CRANKS: CAMPAGNOLO STRADA
SPROCKET: SUGINO CHAINRING (DRILLED) 45T AND CAMPAGNOLO CRANK CAPS
PEDALS: MKS BM-10
CHAIN: HKK SMOKER
HUBS: PHIL WOOD
RIMS: ARAYA 7X
TYRES: MITSUBOSHI COMP III
SEAT: KASHIMAX MX
SEAT POST: RACE INC.
SEAT POST CLAMP: DIA-COMPE TWO-BOLT
BRAKES: SHIMANO TOURNEY DX
LEVERS: SHIMANO TOURNEY DX
GRIPS: A'ME ROUND
EXTRAS: KOOL STOP CONTINENTAL BRAKE PADS, CAMPAGNOLO SUPER RECORD BOTTOM BRACKET, UNION SS SPOKES, SUNTOUR 888 16T FREEWHEEL, BLACK VINYL PADS, HARO TYPE 2 NUMBER PLATE

1981 KUWAHARA KZ-1

SUBMITTED BY **MARK JAMES**

Kuwahara was founded in Osaka, Japan, in 1918 by Sentaro Kuwahara. Initially starting as a small family-run business that made and sold bicycles and parts, the company quickly expanded from its humble roots, and in 1972 Kuwahara shipped its first branded bikes created for the North American, European and Australian markets.

The first BMX model ever made under the Kuwahara brand had no real name and was simply known as the Kuwahara bike. It was a single-gusset frame and was manufactured from 1979 until early 1980. Shown here is the all-time classic KZ-1, Kuwahara's second production model, which improved on the previous frame by being both lighter and stronger, with better geometry for increased handling.

'The trick to building a Kuwahara is just to go all out with Japanese parts,' says the bike's owner, Mark James. 'Concentrate on a few key brands, Suntour, Ukai, OGK, Win, KKT, Dia-Compe and always an Elina seat.'

FRAME: KUWAHARA KZ-1
FORKS: KUWAHARA KZ-1
BARS: WIN
STEM: SUNTOUR POWERSTEM
HEADSET: HATTA
CRANKS: TAKAGI TOURNEY
SPROCKET: TAKAGI
PEDALS: KKT A-MX
CHAIN: IZUMI
HUBS: SR
RIMS: UKAI SPEEDLINE
TYRES: TIOGA COMP III/IV
SEAT: ELINA LIGHTNING BOLT
SEAT POST CLAMP: DIA-COMPE
BRAKE: DIA-COMPE 890
LEVER: DIA-COMPE TECH 2
GRIPS: OGK
EXTRAS: SHIMANO DX FREEWHEEL, DIA-COMPE BRAKE CABLE

1981

MONGOOSE MOTOMAG

SUBMITTED BY **MARK JAMES**

FRAME: TEAM MONGOOSE
FORKS: MONGOOSE COMPETITION
BARS: RACE INC. TYPE
STEM: MONGOOSE
CRANKS: SHIMANO DURA-ACE
PEDALS: KKT K-MX
CHAIN: IZUMI
WHEELS: MONGOOSE MOTOMAG 2
TYRES: CHENG SHIN KNOBBY
SEAT: MONGOOSE SUPER PRO
SEAT POST: FLUTED
SEAT POST CLAMP: MONGOOSE
BRAKE: DIA-COMPE 890
LEVER: PRE-BENT
GRIPS: OURY

When Skip Hess graduated from college with a Bachelor's degree in Mechanical Engineering, he soon found himself working from home as a freelance designer for various car wheel manufacturers. It was at this time that Hess noticed the children in his neighbourhood doing tricks and jumps on their bikes, and the idea of a wheel designed specifically for BMX began to form in his mind.

Shortly after, Hess came up with the first Motomag wheel design and, after a series of knock-backs from manufacturers, decided to start producing the wheels (cast with aluminium alloy) himself. Hess started BMX Products with the help of his friend Bill Miller from his Californian home in September 1974, and his first product was the Motomag 1 wheel.

Sometime between the end of 1975 and early 1976, Hess then trademarked the Mongoose name and logo, inspired by friend and fellow racer Tom 'The Mongoose' McEwen. The production of frames soon followed, and the Motomag was the first Mongoose complete bike to be made. It featured, of course, Motomag wheels, but was also available in a heavy-duty wire wheel option.

1981
DIAMOND BACK SILVER STREAK

SUBMITTED BY **JUAN MATTOS**

FRAME: DIAMOND BACK SILVER STREAK
FORKS: DIAMOND BACK PRO
BARS: DIAMOND BACK MEDIUM
STEM: SR, STAMPED DIAMOND BACK
HEADSET: MX TYPE
CRANKS: SUGINO ONE-PIECE CHROMOLY 175MM
SPROCKET: SUGINO 44T CHAINRING, SUGINO SPIDER
PEDALS: DIAMOND BACK
CHAIN: DIAMOND BACK
RIMS: ARAYA 7X (20 X 1.75)
HUBS: SUZUE LARGE FLANGE
TYRES: DIAMOND BACK IRC: 2.125 FRONT/1.75 REAR
SEAT: DIAMOND BACK AERO
SEAT POST: STRONG FLUTED
SEAT POST CLAMP: SR
BRAKE: DIA-COMPE 890
LEVER: DIA-COMPE TECH III
GRIPS: OAKLEY 3

Diamond Back (DB) was founded in the late 1970s by a small west coast distribution company called Western States Industries (WSI) that originally sold Centurion-branded road bikes but became interested in BMX. DB created this particular bike as an entry-level, affordable, chrome-finished race bike in 1981. DB had planned to reveal the bike for the first time at a BMX race in San Diego, California, in the summer of 1981, where *BMX Action* magazine photographers would be on hand to take photos of it. Sandy Finkleman – owner of local bike shop Wheels 'n Things and also DB's race team manager – reportedly dubbed the bike the Silver Streak just two hours before it went on show for the very first time at the race.

1982
KUWAHARA ET

SUBMITTED BY **LEE MORRIS**

FRAME: KUWAHARA ET
FORKS: KUWAHARA ET
BARS: WIN
STEM: SUGINO
HEADSET: TANGE
CRANKS: SUGINO
SPROCKET: SUGINO
PEDALS: KKT
CHAIN: IZUMI
HUBS: SUZUE
RIMS: UKIA
TYRES: KENDA
SEAT: ELINA LIGHTNING BOLT
SEAT POST: RENTHAL
SEAT POST CLAMP: SUNTOUR
BRAKES: DIA-COMPE 1020
LEVERS: DIA-COMPE TECH 2
GRIPS: KUWAHARA
EXTRAS: ET PAD SET

Japanese manufacturer Kuwahara was propelled to fame after its bikes were featured in *E.T.*, Steven Spielberg's 1982 blockbuster film about a homesick extra terrestrial from a distant planet. The iconic red-and-white colourway that featured on lead character Elliott's bike was created specially for the film.

Universal Studios, the film's producers, entered into an exclusive licensing agreement with Kuwahara (and Everything Bicycles), and after the release of the film Kuwahara started mass production of the ET BMX. Various versions of the bike were created from the original, which featured good Japanese components, a looptail frame and double gussets. The second (the replica), again with a looptail and double gussets, was a slightly more economical version that used less expensive components. The third model was a cheaper Apollo frame model with a single front gusset and non-looptail rear. It was sold in toy shops rather than serious bike shops.

'This bike is built to the US spec (the UK spec had black parts),' explains the bike's owner and restorer Lee Morris. 'I found an ET frame for sale and decided to rebuild the bike. After seeing the US spec with gold parts I decided that was the way to go. Parts came from all over the world via eBay and it took one year to get them all together and finish the bike. Every part was brand new old stock.'

FRAME: HUTCH PRO RACER
FORKS: HUTCH
BARS: HUTCH PRO RACER
STEM: TUF-NECK 2000
HEADSET: TIOGA
CRANKS: MAXY CROSS
SPROCKET: SUGINO
PEDALS: HUTCH BEARTRAP
CHAIN: IZUMI
HUBS: SUNTOUR
RIMS: ACS Z-RIMS
TYRES: TIOGA COMP III
SEAT: KASHIMAX MX
SEAT POST: HUTCH
SEAT POST CLAMP: HUTCH
BRAKE: DC MX-1000
LEVER: DC
GRIPS: OAKLEY B-1B
EXTRAS: TERRYCABLE BRAKE LEVER COVER

1982 HUTCH PRO RACER

SUBMITTED BY **CHRISTOPHER APPOLDT**

Starting out in 1979 as a BMX mail-order company, Hutch founder Richard Hutchins originally began developing his own product line by taking existing-brand products and having them chrome-plated. It didn't take long before Hutchins began developing his own product, however, outsourcing the manufacturing to other established companies such as Profile, Thruster, MCS and VDC.

Promoted as the 'most beautiful bike in the world', the Pro Racer was Hutch's first complete bike and was introduced in 1981. The first edition was completely show-chrome with black parts and retailed for US$419.75, making it one of the most expensive BMX bikes ever produced. It was this bike that secured Hutch's legendary status as the best in BMX.

1982
SE RACING FLOVAL FLYER

SUBMITTED BY **JUAN MATTOS**

As its name suggests, the Floval Flyer was constructed using the same 'floval' aluminium alloy tubing for the top and down tubes that SE's PK Ripper had made famous (see page 58). The Floval Flyer (this particular one was produced around 1982), however, was slightly larger, sporting 24-inch wheels. SE, although no longer owned by its founder Scot Breithaupt, still produces Floval Flyers, with the most recent model released in 2011 (at the time of writing).

1982

HUTCH LIL HOLESHOT

SUBMITTED BY **JUAN MATTOS**

Designed for kids under ten years old, the Hutch LiL Holeshot is a seriously nice little bike. As well as looking the part in shiny chrome, the bike also boasted a number of impressive components, including lightweight aluminium bars, a mini-stem made of magnesium with titanium bolts, and a bearing-free magnesium headset that contains a self-lubricating nylon o-ring.

FRAME: HUTCH LIL HOLESHOT
FORKS: HUTCH LIL HOLESHOT
BARS: HUTCH MINI (ALUMINIUM)
STEM: HUTCH MINI (MAGNESIUM WITH TITANIUM BOLTS)
HEADSET: HUTCH BEARING-FREE SELF-LUBRICATING
CRANKS: HUTCH 170MM HOLLOW ALUMINIUM WITH TITANIUM SPINDLE AND SEALED BARINGS
PEDALS: HUTCH MINI BEARTRAP
HUBS: HUTCH SEALED BEARING

1982 REDLINE PROLINE

SUBMITTED BY **WOODY ITSON**

In 1982 The World Almanac partnered with BMX manufacturers Redline and Skyway to host the World Almanac BMX Skills Competition. 'There were five events you could try and set a world record in,' recalls ex pro freestyle rider Woody Itson. 'What was even better – and not known at the time by the competitors – was that each record setter would win a custom top-of-the-line Redline Proline bike complete with Skyway graphite Tuff wheels, graphite Tuff pedals, and the finned Skyway brake pads. Each bike also came with Oakley 3 grips and a Haro number plate with the winner's name on it.

'This is the actual bike that my good friend Martin Aparijo was given at the 1982 competition for setting the long jump record,' says Itson, who now owns the bike. 'It is all original except the crank decals. The original decals were destroyed because of other stickers being placed over the top of them. It took some time to get it cleaned up and remove some of the rust, but I think it looks awesome. You can see the cracks in the tyres, the scratches on the pedal cages, and the wear to the original decals and seat. But to me this is one really cool survivor to have and a great memory of a simpler time.'

'When I asked Martin why his was still all together and original, a good 27 years after he won it, he said because he had other sponsors, he couldn't really ride it out in public, so his girlfriend rode it around with him on occasion. I actually remember that. One day, he just put it in his garage and there it sat for decades.'

1982
PROFILE CHAMP PRO

SUBMITTED BY **MICHAEL GAMSTETTER**

Profile Racing, Inc. can be traced back to early 1968, when the firm was established by Jim Alley as a race car chassis shop in Flemington, New Jersey. In 1971 Profile moved its operations to St. Petersburg in Florida, and a year later Alley's son and daughter had their first taste of BMX racing. The entire Alley family quickly became hooked on this new sport, and a venture into the bicycle industry was born. With a background in auto racing, chromoly fabrication and lightweight aluminium alloy components, it was an easy transition for Profile to make.

1979 was the year Profile produced its first three-piece chromoly tubular crank set, which went on to become an industry standard for BMX. One year later, in 1980, Profile produced the Champ, their first lightweight chromoly frame set. The Champ featured a large-diameter down tube (a concept still used in frame building today) plus an extra (half-inch) smaller tube which triangulated the long frame front – a combination that made the frame extremely rigid and distinctive.

FRAME: PROFILE CHAMP PRO
FORKS: PROFILE CHAMP PRO
BARS: GT PRO
STEM: DK
HEADSET: OMAS
CRANKS: PROFILE SECOND-GENERATION 175
SPROCKET: PHIL WOOD 130-BCD SPIDER AND PETE'S PRECISION CHAINRING 45T
PEDALS: SUNTOUR
CHAIN: SEDIS SPORT
HUBS: CAMPAGNOLO TIPPO FRONT AND OMAS REAR
RIMS: AMBROSSIO
TYRES: TIOGA COMP III REPRODUCTIONS, 20 X 2.125 FRONT, 20 X 1.75 REAR
SEAT: KASHIMAX AERO
SEAT POST: CHROMOLY
SEAT POST CLAMP: DIA-COMPE HINGED
BRAKE: DIA-COMPE MX 1000
LEVER: DIA-COMPE TECH 3
GRIPS: OAKLEY 2010 B1B
EXTRAS: KOOL-STOP CONTINENTAL BRAKE PADS, SS UNION SPOKES WITH BRASS NIPPLES, PROFILE BOTTOM BRACKET, SHIMANO 333 16T FREEWHEEL, CALIFORNIA LITE STEM AND BAR PADS (NOS), NEAL NUMBER PLATE

1982 TORKER 280X

SUBMITTED BY **MARK JAMES**

FRAME: TORKER 280X
FORKS: TORKER
BARS: TORKER PRO T
STEM: SR MS-420
HEADSET: TANGE AW-27
CRANKS: SUGINO OPC
SPROCKET: SUGINO SPIDER AND CHAINRING
PEDALS: MKS BM-10
CHAIN: D.I.D.
HUBS: SUNTOUR
RIMS: ARAYA 7X
TYRES: PANARACER KNARLER KNOBBY
SEAT: TORKER (ARIAKE)
SEAT POST: SR
SEAT POST CLAMP: SR
BRAKE: DIA-COMPE 890
LEVER: DIA-COMPE TECH 2
GRIPS: A'ME TRI
EXTRAS: SUNTOUR FREEWHEEL, DIA-COMPE BRAKE CABLE

Torker started out in 1975 as a family business operating from a small garage in California. Founded by John Johnson (and originally named Texon), the company soon became famous for its quality frame engineering – including the famous twin top tube design, which was created to make manufacturing easier.

In 1982 Torker began to chase a new niche in the BMX market. As many serious BMX racers were custom building their own high-end race bikes, retailers were asking for less-expensive bikes to meet the growing demand from kids who wanted bikes at a lower price. For Torker, this meant the introduction of the 280X, whose name came from the suggested retail price of US$280. In order to meet this price point, Shimano and Torker components were replaced with cheaper Sugino and Sakae Ringyo (SR) parts.

'This 280X is my best survivor find out of 90 bikes and eight years of collecting,' says Mark James. 'They're a nightmare to pick up in a decent condition without the original chrome beaten up and sprayed over, but this looks like it came out of the box yesterday. Even though it's a basic mid-budget bike, the condition and, I guess, its authenticity as a real street bike, is its appeal.'

1982
RALEIGH TUFF BURNER

SUBMITTED BY **DAVE HALL**

FRAME: RALEIGH BURNER
FORKS: RALEIGH BURNER
STEM: SR
WHEELS: SKYWAY TUFF II
TYRES: TIOGA COMP III
BRAKES: WEINMANN
LEVERS: WEINMANN
EXTRAS: VINYL PAD SET

This bike is owned by Dave Hall, a collector of 36 years with a passion for the old British BMX icon: the humble and sometimes maligned Raleigh Burner. Hall explains: 'I had a MK1 Raleigh Extra Burner as a boy, receiving it in 1983 at the age of 10. I rode that bike to death, covering countless miles in my attempt to emulate my heroes Andy Ruffell and Craig Schofield of Team Raleigh.'

Fast forward approximately 25 years and Hall is now known as the biggest Raleigh Burner enthusiast in the UK. He runs the website burnerworld.co.uk and organizes the annual Raleigh Burner show, The Burner Bash.

First launched in 1982, Raleigh Burners were originally a replacement for the Grifter. Possibly the most iconic British bike from the early days of 1980s BMX, the Tuff Burner wasn't the most technically advanced bike, but with its distinctive colour scheme (and Skyway Tuff wheels that inspired the bike's name) it is the one model that everyone remembers.

1982

SE RACING PK RIPPER

SUBMITTED BY **JUAN MATTOS**

The PK Ripper is, quite simply, one of the best known BMX bikes of all time. Its designer, Scot Breithaupt of SE Racing, came up with the idea of 'floval' tubing where instead of being round, the tubes are flat on the sides and rounded top and bottom in a kind of flat oval shape – hence the name. Breithaupt also invested in pioneering aluminium-welding techniques to enable the PK Ripper to be the first successful aluminium alloy (made with 6061-T6 alloy) BMX frame, making it lighter than most frames available at the time.

The design, Breithaupt has stated in various interviews, took much trial and error to perfect and was, in fact, an updated version of SE Racing's JU-6 bike (see page 32). The JU-6 was designed for and named after SE team rider Jeff Utterback in honour of his number six place in the national rankings in 1977. However, Utterback's father set up his own company GJS (see page 36), so Jeff soon left SE to ride for the family company. A gusset was added to the JU-6 design alongside a few other small changes and the PK Ripper, named after SE team rider and race winner Perry Kramer, was born. The combination of ahead-of-its time design and Breithaupt's undoubted promotional and marketing prowess, meant that SE had orders of over 2,000 units for the PK Ripper before the company had shipped even a single frame.

1982
DIAMOND BACK TURBO

SUBMITTED BY **JUAN MATTOS**

Rider Harry Leary had already had a bike made specially for him in 1975 by his then sponsors JMC (see page 24). But Leary quit JMC soon after and was then sponsored by Diamond Back, who manufactured the Turbo in 1982 – Turbo being Leary's nickname as he had 'turboed' himself into second place in both the ABA and NBL rankings in 1981.

Leary stayed with Diamond Back until 1992, becoming the manufacturer's racing team manager in October 1986.

This particular bike was found as new old stock (NOS) by Jeff Haney at a bike shop years ago. It was built up, although a few components had been sold before collector Juan Mattos got hold of it in 2007.

Juan Mattos is also the owner of this amazing one-off Diamond Back Turbo pit bike, custom built by C4 Labs in Delaware, USA. A pit bike is a smaller (16-inch-wheel) version of a standard BMX (20-inch-wheel) bike. Like most things BMX, they were originally inspired by motorcycle pit bikes, which were used for riding around the pits or staging area of a motocross race. Pit BMX bikes with extra-long seat posts and oversized handlebars soon became a popular sight at BMX events in the 1980s.

1983
JMC CRUISER

SUBMITTED BY **JUAN MATTOS**

JMC built 24-inch cruisers between 1982 and 1985, producing just 452 in that time. Of those, only 30 were made in black, making this particular bike, put together by Jeff Haney from a new-old-stock frame and fork set, incredibly rare. There were also a small number of frames made in candy-apple red, candy blue and just three were finished in white. The vast majority of these mid-1980s JMC cruisers were made with a chrome finish.

'Darrell Young was more than likely the best-known rider to ride one of these,' recalls Jim Melton (the JM in JMC). 'He rode the first one unpainted and then the next one he had was candy-apple red. Most of the JMC team at the time had and rode them.'

1983
SE RACING QUADANGLE

SUBMITTED BY **CHRISTOPHER APPOLDT**

Another innovative design from SE Racing, the Quadangle is well-known for its highly distinctive frame configuration with four different triangles (the clue's in the name). These triangles create an inverted headtube (where the top tube joins the steering headtube below the twin down tubes).

The majority of stress on the headtube occurs at the bottom (usually where the down tube joins up), so the thinking behind the design was that the thicker crossbar should join the headtube where it is put under the most stress, and the thinner twin down tubes should join where it's under less stress.

The first Quadangles (from 1979 to 1982) were originally built as looptails, but the design changed in 1982 to feature more standard dropouts. One other thing to note is that the seat post clamp on this bike is reversed, because SE slotted the seat post mast in the front, not the rear.

'Every part of this bike, aside from innertubes and grease, is new old-school stock,' explains the bike's owner Christopher Appoldt.

FRAME: SE RACING QUADANGLE
FORKS: LANDING GEAR (NO STAMP ON FORK BOTTOMS)
BARS: POWERLITE POWERBENDS
STEM: SUNTOUR
HEADSET: TANGE 125
CRANKS: SUNTOUR VX
SPROCKET: SUNTOUR
PEDALS: SHIMANO SX
CHAIN: IZUMI
HUBS: SUNTOUR
RIMS: ARAYA 7X
TYRES: TIOGA COMP IV FAT/SKINNY
SEAT: KASHIMAX AERO
SEAT POST: FLUTED
SEAT POST CLAMP: SUNTOUR
BRAKE: DIA-COMPE MX-1000
LEVER: DIA-COMPE MX-1000
GRIPS: OAKLEY F-1
EXTRAS: SE RACING QUADANGLE PAD SET

FRAME: PATTERSON PR240
FORKS: BOTTEMA RACE
BARS: GT CRUISER
STEM: PRO NECK
CRANKS: PROFILE
PEDALS: SHIMANO DX
HUBS: BULLSEYE
RIMS: ARAYA 7X
TYRES: TIOGA COMP III
SEAT: KASHIMAX MX
SEAT POST: PATTERSON
SEAT POST CLAMP: DIA-COMPE MX
BRAKE: SHIMANO DX
LEVER: SHIMANO DX
GRIPS: A'ME ROUND
EXTRAS: UNI NUMBER PLATE, DICE CAPS

1983
PATTERSON PR240 CRUISER

SUBMITTED BY **ANDREAS STEVENS**

Originally founded in 1977 by Vance Patterson (father of pro racers Brent and Brian Patterson), Patterson Racing manufactured frames, forks, bars, seat posts and was known for its state-of-the-art geometry.

Keeping things in the family, Patterson also had a strong racing team in the form of brothers Brent and Brian; the only brothers to both hold the national number one pro title in any major BMX sanctioning body. Brent held the ABA's National No. 1 Pro title in 1980, but in 1982 had to settle for the No. 2 slot as his brother Brian took the No. 1 title that year, and also again in 1983.

The bike shown here is a PR240 Cruiser featuring custom yellow paintwork, with Bottema race forks, GT cruiser bars and Profile cranks.

1983
NOMURA

SUBMITTED BY **JUAN MATTOS**

In 1979 motocross racer Wade Nomura set up a small bike shop called Nomura Racing Products in Santa Barbara, California. While designing for various BMX manufacturers to pay the bills, he worked on perfecting his own 20-inch aluminium frame design. Nomura was obsessed by its geometry – even collaborating with his orthopaedic surgeon uncle to try to calculate the perfect steering-tube angle, while utilizing maximum pulling power on the handlebars. Only 525 Nomura frames were ever built, 313 of those were 20-inch aluminium frames and survivors are few and far between. The frames were built by True Radius Bending (TRB), a company also local to Santa Barbara that was, at the time, working on NASA's Space Shuttle project. TRB's aluminium welders were reputed to be the best in the land at that time.

1983
SKYWAY TA

SUBMITTED BY **MARK JAMES**

Skyway started in 1963 as a machine shop in Glendale, California. The name came from an airport across the street and the very first products they manufactured were for the aerospace industry.

When BMX began to emerge in southern California, Skyway made probably its most famous contribution to the sport in the form of a 20-inch nylon 'mag' wheel.

Then came the TA, a beautiful frame and fork set which utilized an unusual teardrop-shaped chromoly tubing. A long time in development, it was this tubing that inspired the name TA, which stands for Totally Aerodynamic.

'My TA is based on the iconic 1984 Skyway Street Thrashin' advert, albeit now with black Tuffs,' says Mark James. 'It was my first dream bike and I stared endlessly at the back cover of UK magazine *BMX Action Bike* (not to be confused with US *BMX Action*). Everyone wanted to be the kid in the ad, cruising the streets of California.'

FRAME: SKYWAY TA
FORKS: SKYWAY TA
BARS: CW PRO
STEM: SUNTOUR MS-1100
HEADSET: HATTA
CRANKS: SUGINO OPC
SPROCKET: SR SPIDER, SUGINO CHAINRING
PEDALS: SKYWAY TUFF
CHAIN: IZUMI
WHEELS: SKYWAY TUFF II
TYRES: PANARACER FREESTYLE
SEAT: SHOTGUN II
SEAT POST: CW
SEAT POST CLAMP: DIA-COMPE
BRAKE: DIA-COMPE MX1000
LEVER: DIA-COMPE TECH 3
GRIPS: A'ME UNITRON
EXTRAS: DIA-COMPE BRAKE CABLE, SKYWAY CAL-LITE PAD SET

FRAME: HARO FREESTYLER
FORKS: HARO FREESTYLE
BARS/STEM: VECTOR
HEADSET: YST
CRANKS: REDLINE 401
SPROCKET: REDLINE 401
PEDALS: SHIMANO DX
CHAIN: IZUMI
WHEELS: SKYWAY GRAPHITE TUFF II
TYRES: TIOGA COMP III
SEAT: KASHIMAX
SEAT POST: ANLUN
SEAT POST CLAMP: DIA-COMPE MX
BRAKES: DIA-COMPE MX1000
LEVERS: DIA-COMPE TECH 4
GRIPS: A'ME TRI
EXTRAS: REDLINE TECHMATIC BOTTOM BRACKET, SUNTOUR COASTER

1983 HARO FREESTYLER

SUBMITTED BY **JOHN BUULTJENS**

Possibly the most famous name in BMX, Bob Haro started his involvement in the sport in the 1970s creating numbers for racers to use on their number plates. They became so popular that he eventually started selling them, and Haro's artistic flair went on to help him start his own company and branch into making products, the first of which were plastic number plates.

Haro was also a brilliant and inventive BMX rider, who rode for Torker in the late 1970s and early 1980s. Haro was certainly one of the earliest pioneers of freestyle (another outlet for his creativity), and in 1981 he approached Torker to help him develop and build the very first purpose-built freestyle frame set.

Unveiled in 1982, the Haro Freestyler was manufactured by Torker, but designed, developed and marketed by Bob Haro's new enterprise: Haro Bikes. It was a totally new concept in BMX, the first frame and fork kit designed specifically for freestyle. Available in chrome only, the design included innovative features such as an integrated coaster brake bracket and freestyle-specific geometry.

The bike shown here is owned by serious Haro collector 'Scottish' John Buultjens. 'It all started ten years ago when my folks back in Scotland were moving house,' explains Buultjens. 'They packed up all my things [and] shipped them to me in Australia. I was so stoked to receive all my old broken Haros from the '80s. It was then that I decided to rebuild them. I wanted all my memories to come back to life.'

With almost 20 bikes, Buultjens' collection includes every Haro pro model from 1982 to 1991, and he prizes his collection so highly it is insured for AUS$100,000.

As well as his passion for all things Haro, in 2010 Buultjens started up his own BMX brand based in Australia, which is called Pilgrim.

1983

PRO NECK NATIONAL PRO STANDARD

SUBMITTED BY **JUAN MATTOS**

Pro Neck was a company created specifically to sell Pro Neck stems, designed and manufactured by a company called Bakton Enterprises. The company ended up selling frames, forks, bars, stems, sprockets and other parts and accessories, but its National Pro race-specific frames were distinctive for the tubular gusset support which ran between the bottom and top tubes, in parallel with the headtube.

1983
CW PHAZE 1 (TEAM ISSUE)

SUBMITTED BY **JUAN MATTOS**

Custom Works (CW) Racing sponsored then 14-year-old amateur BMX rider Billy Griggs from January to December 1983. This particular frame is Griggs' original frame set and has the serial number 'Billy Griggs'. In addition to the custom serial number, the frame can be identified by double-thick dropouts and a steeper headtube angle. The frame set is apparently one of two made; the other was given to factory rider Tracer Finn at the time of Griggs' departure from the team.

1984
CW PHAZE 1 CRUISER

SUBMITTED BY **JUAN MATTOS**

Originally in white when he bought it, BMX enthusiast Jeff Haney stripped back the frame and repowdered it in red. The sticker that says Phaze 1 was missing so a replica was specially made. This bike is one of only a handful known to exist.

1984
TORKER FREESTYLE PROTOTYPE

SUBMITTED BY **WOODY ITSON**

FRAME: TORKER FREESTYLE PROTOTYPE #1
FORKS: TORKER FREESTYLE PROTOTYPE #1
BARS: WOODY ITSON FREESTYLE BARS BY VDC, FIRST GENERATION
STEM: PRO NECK (MARTIN APARIJO'S ORIGINAL STEM)
CRANKS: REDLINE FLIGHT 170MM
SPROCKET: REDLINE 41T
PEDALS: HUTCH WITH HUTCH FS CAGES
CHAIN: IZUMI
HUBS: SST GEN 1-S (TEAM ISSUE)
RIMS: MONGOOSE PRO CLASS
TYRES: MISTUBOSHI COMP III 20 X 2.175
SEAT: KASHIMAX AERO
SEAT POST: SST COMMAND POST (FROM BRIAN SCURA)
SEAT POST CLAMP: SR (APARIJO'S ORIGINAL CLAMP)
BRAKES: DIA-COMPE MX 900
LEVERS: DIA-COMPE TECH 3
GRIPS: A'ME UNITRONS
EXTRAS: MAX SEAT COVER, SUNTOUR 16T FREEWHEEL

'This is the first Torker freestyle frame built under the Torker brand name,' explains Woody Itson, who lovingly restored the bike in 2009 after getting the frame and forks from its designer and original owner, early freestyle pioneer, Martin Aparijo. 'This is the only Torker FS frame made with a 4-inch headtube,' Itson continues. A later prototype, also owned by Itson, was built with a 5-inch headtube. 'The frame was finished in its original colour and built to the same specs that Martin had it built to back in 1984. Martin rode this bike with red and black components due to his ties with Vans but I wanted to build it in true Torker colours so went with gold and black.'

1984
GJS FREESTYLER PROTOTYPE

SUBMITTED BY **JUAN MATTOS**

FRAME: GJS FREESTYLER PROTOTYPE
FORKS: GJS
BARS: POWER BEND
STEM: HUTCH
HEADSET: TANGE 125
CRANKS: HUTCH AERO SPEED 180MM
CHAINRING: SUGINO 42T
PEDALS: HUTCH BEARTRAP
CHAIN: IZUMI
WHEELS: ARAYA 7X
HUBS: SST SUPERLACE 2ND GEN
TYRES: COMP III STADIUM
SEAT: CYCLE PRO SHOT GUN II
SEAT POST: SST COMMAND
SEAT POST CLAMP: HUTCH
BRAKES: FRONT: DIA-COMPE MX 900, REAR: MX1000
GRIPS: OAKLEY B-1B

This is the very first GJS Freestyler ever made and the only one with triple top tubes. It's been lovingly restored by collector Juan Mattos, who had to remove no fewer than six layers of paint and chrome, restore the dropouts and remove a few dents before giving it three new coats of chrome for a jaw-dropping finish. Chip Bowers from C4 Labs took several attempts to get a perfect paint finish in candy red. The result speaks for itself. Mattos then built the bike up several times, trying different components and colour combinations before finally settling on the build shown. It won both the Best of Freestyle and the Best of Show awards at the annual Rockford Collector's Gathering in 2009.

FRAME: GT PRO PERFORMER
FORKS: GT PRO PERFORMER
BARS: GT PRO RACE
STEM: TUF-NECK
HEADSET: TIOGA
CRANKS: SUGINO ONE-PIECE
SPROCKET: TUF-NECK UNSTAMPED POWERDISC AND CHAINRING
PEDALS: SHIMANO DX
CHAIN: IZUMI
WHEELS: SKYWAY TUFF II
TYRES: GT FREESTYLE
SEAT: KASHIMAX MX
SEAT POST: GT LAIDBACK
SEAT POST CLAMP: TUF-NECK
BRAKES: DIA-COMPE MX1000
LEVERS: DIA-COMPE TECH 3
GRIPS: A'ME ROUND
EXTRAS: GT PADSET

1984
GT PRO PERFORMER

SUBMITTED BY **CARL TURNER**

Gary Turner was an early pioneer of BMX manufacturing. Having been a welder working on drag racing cars in the 1960s, he started to modify and customize bikes for his son to ride in the early 1970s. In 1973 he built his son a frame to ride on the sun-soaked tracks of southern California. Soon after Turner teamed up with Richard Long and GT Bicycles was born, with Turner designing and building some of the most innovative frames in BMX and Long handling the business side: selling, promoting and sponsoring riders.

In 1983 two of freestyle BMX's early pioneers and founders of the American Freestyle Association (AFA), Eddie Fiola and Bob Morales, finished contracts with Kuwahara. (The previous year Fiola had spent time promoting Kuwahara's ET bike.) They both signed to GT. Together with Gary Turner they designed the first GT freestyle frame and named it the GT Performer. It came out in 1984, the year Fiola took first place in the pro category at both the 'King of the Skateparks' event (with a broken wrist in a cast) and the AFA Freestyle Championships. 1984 is also the year he travelled to the UK to compete in the Kelloggs TV BMX Championships, a hugely popular TV show hosted by Mick Brown and Andy Ruffell. Brown and Ruffell dubbed him the 'Flying Banana' and the nickname stuck. Fiola was at the top of freestyle around this time, appearing on numerous magazine front covers, usually airborn.

This particular Eddie Fiola replica was voted Best Freestyle Bike at the Bournemouth Show and Shine in 2005. 'I've recently added the black pads and black laidback GT seat post without the GT roundel sticker exactly as Fiola rode back in '84,' explains its owner Carl Turner. 'It was a bike built by Jason Eley and I added the finishing touches.' Turner began riding in 1979 on a Puch Murray 360 and continued until 1987 competing in both racing and freestyle competitions. 'I still race at the RADBMX national meets and still with my old race number of 306. The Fiola replica is just one of many in my collection now, alongside a restored Puch Murray and a Diamond Back Turbo.'

1984

FREE AGENT FREE FLIGHT FREESTYLE

SUBMITTED BY **JUAN MATTOS**

Yet another show-winning restoration of an old-school BMX bike from the collection of Juan Mattos. Free Agent was originally started by Voris Dixon of VDC, but in 1984 he sold it to the family of Brent Shoup, Californian BMX rider. Note the way the top tube appears to stick straight through the headtube – a bit of a Voris Dixon design give-away (see page 72).

In the early 1990s KHS bought the Free Agent brand name and they continue to produce Free Agent bikes and accessories today.

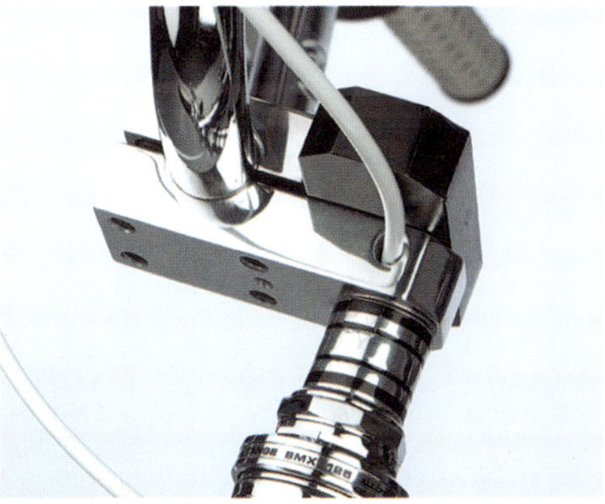

1984

VDC CHANGA

SUBMITTED BY **JUAN MATTOS**

Voris Dixon got into BMX in the mid 1970s by sponsoring riders through Bikeland, the shop he co-owned in Anaheim, California.

Dixon set up a bike parts manufacturing company with Vaughn Bandoian called B&D Sales (Bandoian & Dixon), before setting up Voris Dixon Company (VDC) in 1976 in Santa Anna, California. VDC made components such as frames, forks, bars and seat posts for BMX companies, including GT, Pro Neck, Traker, Vector, Two Wheeler, Hutch and Robinson, before starting its own line of bikes. The best known of its bikes is the Changa, of which the prototype was released in 1982. VDC frames featured a unique and easily recognizable dual headtube piercing design and used a 5-inch headtube with a road-bike-sized headset.

The chrome-finished VDC Changa was available as a chromoly frame set (frame and forks) that was packaged with pads and headset. It was designed as a lightweight race-winner and UK magazine *BMX Bi-Weekly* noted that when they tested it for review (issue 12, volume 3), the complete bike weighed 10.5 kg (just over 23lbs).

1984

VDC CHANGA FREESTYLE

SUBMITTED BY **JUAN MATTOS**

Like the Changa race bike, the Changa Freestyle was available in frame and fork sets. The frame had been tweaked to stand up to the slightly different needs of the freestyler. The most obvious differences being the double down tubes and a slightly steeper headtube angle. There were other aspects of the frame that set it apart from the competition too. When the bike was tested by *Freestyle BMX* magazine (issue 14, volume 1), the reviewer noted that the rear seat and chainstays were formed from ¾-inch tubing rather than the more usual ⅝-inch. 'Now that's talking TOUGH,' the reviewer remarked before also observing that the rear dropouts were twice as thick as most other BMX dropouts at a full ¼ inch, making them super-stiff and extra durable.

VDC actually made most of its money manufacturing components, including forks, alloy bars and alloy seat posts for other BMX companies. In 2009 the company re-emerged as a manufacturer of BMX frames and released the Changa II, which features the recognizable double pierced headtube.

1984
RICKMAN FREESTYLER

SUBMITTED BY **RAVI KAJLA**

FRAME: RICKMAN FREESTYLER
FORKS: RICKMAN FREESTYLE
BARS: RICKMAN FREESTYLE
STEM: REDLINE FORKLIFTER
CRANKS: TIOGA CR-MO TUBULAR MAX-FLO
SPROCKET: SUGINO
PEDALS: SHIMANO PD-MX15
WHEELS: SKYWAY TUFF II
TYRES: PANARACER FREESTYLE
SEAT: ELINA FLYTE-TECH
SEAT POST: HSIN LUNG
SEAT POST CLAMP: HUTCH DONUT
BRAKES: DIA-COMPE MX
LEVERS: DIA-COMPE 283 TECH-V
GRIPS: A'ME ROUND
EXTRAS: DICE VALVE CAPS

Rickman Bros. was a hugely successful Hampshire-based UK motorcycle manufacturing company set up in the early 1960s by motocross racing brothers Don and Derek Rickman. In the 1980s the brothers sold their company and licensed the Rickman name to motorbike rider and enthusiast Adrian Moss, who continued to run the Rickman Engineering factory in New Milton in the New Forest, UK. The company made BMX bike frames and parts for Curtis and also for March Racing Developments (MRD) under fabrication agreements in the early 1980s.

Because of the Rickman company's heritage and knowledge of building motorbike frames out of high-quality Reynolds 531 tubing (a British-patented manganese-molybdenum, medium-carbon steel bicycle tubing), the BMX bikes produced by the factory were of extremely high quality.

The Rickman Freestyler is considered one of the best UK-made freestyle bikes of the 1980s and it was, when released in 1984, more expensive than the other UK freestyle frame available at the time, the DP Firebird Freestyler (see page 77). These are now quite rare and feature neat brazed welding in the joints, elegant geometry with a down tube similar to that of a GT Performer (see page 70), and slender twin top tubes rather like those of the Haro Freestyler (see page 65).

This particular bike was bought from a guy called Tom, who reluctantly had to sell the parts of his dream old-school build for financial reasons. Originally sporting a chrome finish, this Rickman frame and forks were stripped and repowdered in white before being built back up. Now it is hardly ridden but kept as an art object by its current owner.

FRAME: CURTIS PRO
FORKS: CURTIS PRO
BARS: CURTIS PRO
STEM: TUF-NECK
HEADSET: TIOGA MX BEARTRAP
CRANKS: SUGINO ONE-PIECE
SPROCKET: SUGINO SPIDER AND CHAINRING
PEDALS: SHIMANO DX
CHAIN: IZUMI
RIMS: ARAYA SHINEY SIDE
TYRES: COMP III
SEAT: KASHIMAX MX
SEAT POST: CURTIS
SEAT POST CLAMP: SUNTOUR
BRAKE: DIA-COMPE MX1000
LEVER: DIA-COMPE TECH 3
GRIPS: A'ME BUBBLE FRONT
EXTRAS: CUSTOM PAD SET, TIOGA BOTTOM BRACKET

1984 CURTIS PRO

SUBMITTED BY **NICK WILSON**

Brian Curtis was originally a well-known British motocross rider back in the 1960s, who started off his frame-building career with a motocross brand called Rickman (see page 73). Honing his skills further, Curtis then went on to make his own Curtis/Honda motocross bikes, with a Curtis built frame and swing arm, and Honda running gear.

Curtis met Gary Woodhouse towards the end of the 1970s, and Woodhouse convinced him to start building BMX frames. This advice changed everything for Curtis, who then stopped making motorbikes and started concentrating solely on pedal bikes.

Woodhouse eventually ended up taking control of the company, but to this day Curtis still oversees the welding on everything produced by the Curtis Bikes company, with all frames hand-built in a workshop in Wiltshire, UK.

Submitted by Nick Wilson, the bike shown here is a classic all-chrome and black Curtis Pro race bike. Wilson also owns a number of other Curtis bikes, including a rare 1986 Brian Curtis Expert.

1984
RALEIGH AERO PRO BURNER

SUBMITTED BY **DAVE HALL**

When Raleigh released its 1984 range of Burners, this bike was the flagship model. With oval tubing, race-specification geometry, plus high-quality components such as sealed-bearing Suntour hubs and Araya Aero rims, this was the Burner fan's dream bike.

'As a lad in a small village in Nottinghamshire I could only dream of owning one of these bikes,' says Dave Hall. 'Nobody I knew ever owned one and the closest I ever got was drooling over one in the local Raleigh dealership.' It has taken Hall 25 years to finally get his hands on one and, now fully restored, it is one of his most prized bikes.

FRAME: TANGE
FORKS: TANGE
BARS: AERO PRO
STEM: SUNTOUR POWER STEM
HEADSET: TANGE 300
CRANKS: SUGINO
SPROCKET: SUGINO 44T
PEDALS: SR CUSTOM M
CHAIN: IZUMI
HUBS: SUNTOUR
RIMS: ARAYA AERO
TYRES: COMP III
SEAT: KASHIMAX AERO
SEAT POST: TANGE
SEAT POST CLAMP: SUNTOUR
BRAKES: DIA-COMPE MX900
LEVERS: DIA-COMPE TECH 3
GRIPS: TANGE
EXTRAS: LIGHTWEIGHT PAD SET

1984
REDLINE RL-20 PRO-STYLER

SUBMITTED BY **JUAN MATTOS**

When Redline signed freestyle pioneer R.L. Osborn early in 1983, the brand started working on a bike which they prototyped for the rider so that he could have input on the design. The result was this bike; the RL in its title referring to the rider's name. The frame has a thick oval down tube and the top tube is butted at each end meaning it is thick at the seat tube end, thinner in the middle, then thicker at the headtube where it is under most stress. This gives the bike such strength that Redline warrantied each RL-20 Pro-Styler frame and fork for a lifetime. The frame also boasts Redline's 5-inch headtube rather than the more usual 4-inch length, adding greater frame rigidity.

The tapered forks came with threaded inserts on both sides for the removable standing pegs that Redline was working on at the time of release. On the back of the top of the forks there are brazed-on cable guides for the front brake cable to clip neatly into. Both are nice touches.

It should be noted that the bike pictured here is not shown exactly how the RL-20 Pro-Styler was first sold. It was originally sold as a complete bike sporting Redline STR bars, Redline Forklifter stem, Hatta MX-II headset, Peregrine wheels (as pictured on this bike), National Panaracer Freestyle tyres, Dia-Compe brakes, KKT RMX Pedals, Sugino one-piece cranks, Hatta bottom bracket, Sugino steel chainwheel (44 teeth) and Sugino A5 spider with a Suntour 16 teeth rear sprocket.

1984
REDLINE PL-20 CARRERA

SUBMITTED BY **JUAN MATTOS**

The PL stands for Pro Line – Redline's bikes aimed at BMX pros or full-sized (adult) riders. This bike, the PL-20 Carrera, was launched in 1982 and had been designed specifically for pro rider Stu Thomsen. It was sold as a complete bike and the bike pictured here is pretty accurate in terms of the components that were originally featured.

Originally the bike came with a Redline PL-20 chromoly frame and forks with Redline V-bars, chromoly seat post, Suntour alloy seat post clamp, chromed-steel headset, Redline aluminium 4-bolt clamp stem with a chromoly shaft, Redline tubular chromoly cranks (401 series), sealed bottom bracket, Redline 44T sprocket, KKT Lightning pedals, Suntour hubs, chrome-plated spokes, Ukai 36-hole wheel rims, Dia-Compe MX1000 brakes with Dia-Compe touring levers and cables, Oakley .5 grips and a set of three Redline pads.

1984
DP FIREBIRD FREESTYLER

SUBMITTED BY **IAIN BOWDEN**

FRAME: DP FIREBIRD FREESTYLER
FORKS: DP FIREBIRD FREESTYLER
BARS: CW PRO
STEM: SR
HEADSET: TIOGA MX-600
CRANKS: SUGINO ONE-PIECE
SPROCKET: SUGINO 44T WITH SUGINO SPIDER AND BOLTS
PEDALS: MKS BM-10 FOOTJAW
CHAIN: IZUMI
HUBS: ACS Z-HUBS
RIMS: ACS Z-RIMS
TYRES: KENDA WHITEWALL
SEAT: KASHIMAX AERO
SEAT POST: GT LAYBACK
SEAT POST CLAMP: TUF-NECK
BRAKES: DIA-COMPE 890
LEVERS: DIA-COMPE TECH 3
GRIPS: A'ME TRI
EXTRAS: TIOGA SEALED BOTTOM BRACKET, SHIMANO 16T FREEWHEEL

UK resident and keen cyclist Dave Park bought every cycling magazine he could find to while away a few hours at a Dutch airport one day in 1981. One of the magazines, *Fiet-Cross*, was a BMX magazine and Park found himself hooked. He was puzzled by the fact that no UK manufacturer was producing high-quality chromoly TIG-welded frame sets like the Americans and the Japanese. So, after much design work and experimentation with welding methods, he set up his own bike manufacturing company, DP Racing, with a small factory in Warrington, UK. The DP Firebird was the first frame set made by the company; it reached the market in 1982. The Mini Firebird and the Delta II frames followed before DP released the Firebird Freestyler with its double top tubes and super-beefy rear dropouts. It was beautifully made with impressively strong and neat welding, yet was affordably priced. Frame sets cost just £75. This bike was justifiably the bestselling freestyle BMX in Britain in the mid 1980s. The DP factory, which had subsequently moved to north Wales, closed in 1987.

'I have owned 14 DPs over the years now,' says Iain Bowden. 'I still own four, which I am keeping. I just have such great memories from the early [to] mid '80s with my Firebird. I think that's why I love them so much.'

1984

HUTCH PRO STAR

SUBMITTED BY **MARK JAMES**

The Hutch Pro Star retailed in the UK for £1,200 (the most expensive factory-produced BMX at the time), so inevitably it was the ultimate dream bike – and it was beyond the depths of most parents' pockets. It was the no-expense-spared BMX, using all Hutch's top components (such as its beartrap pedals, deep-H stem and Aerospeed cranks), which utilized exotic materials such as aircraft aluminium, magnesium and titanium.

The name Hutch will forever be synonymous with ultimate quality, design and engineering. It was actually the Hutch Pro Racer frame that was used to create the Pro Star, but only the highest-quality frames were hand-picked by Hutch for the best welding and perfect chrome finish.

'Hutch continues to command a premium price among collectors,' says Mark James. 'On eBay this could easily cost £5,000 to build today, even the grips can cost over £500!'

James also built a matching Hutch Trick Star, creating an amazing pair of premium BMX bikes. To find out more about James' bikes, see our interview with him on page 146.

FRAME: HUTCH PRO STAR
FORKS: HUTCH PRO STAR
BARS: HUTCH PRO
STEM: HUTCH DEEP H
HEADSET: TANGE MX125
CRANKS: HUTCH AEROSPEED
SPROCKET: HUTCH AEROSPEED WITH TAKAGI 43T CHAINRING
PEDALS: HUTCH PRO BEARTRAP
CHAIN: IZUMI
HUBS: HUTCH
RIMS: ARAYA 7X
TYRES: MITSUBOSHI COMP IV
SEAT: HUTCH KASHIMAX
SEAT POST: HUTCH
SEAT POST CLAMP: HUTCH DONUT
BRAKE: DIA-COMPE MX1000
LEVER: DIA-COMPE TECH 3
GRIPS: HUTCH
EXTRAS: HUTCH 2N1 HEADSET LOCK, HUTCH PAD SET, SHIMANO DX FREEWHEEL, HUTCH RAD KAPS, HUTCH NUMBER PLATE

1985
HUTCH THE JUDGE

SUBMITTED BY **JUAN MATTOS**

The Judge is a race bike named after Florida-born BMX rider Tim 'Da Judge' Judge, who was renowned for performing innovative jumps and tricks while airborn. Hutch sponsored Judge from 1981 to late 1985 and The Judge frame and fork set was released in 1985.

The bike has a notably steep steering headtube angle at 74.5 degrees. This makes for snappy steering. The seat tube angle is also steeper than the Hollywood frame that Hutch brought out around the same time. The Judge boasted thick tabs on the forks and on the rear dropouts – as thick as on the manufacturer's freestyle Trick Star bike (see pages 80–83). This meant less flex, extra stiffness and all round more durability.

'For a long time I wanted a bike that steered faster,' said Tim Judge in a piece in *BMX Action* magazine's April issue in 1985. 'It works. It's great man,' he continues. 'You just sit back, aim it where you want, and hold on. It jumps up a storm, boy. No doubt. The old Pro Racer jumped good, but I did a couple [of] things to this one so I'd be able to do even more. I just wanted to be able to hit a jump and hang out in the air for a while.'

FRAME: HUTCH THE JUDGE
FORKS: HUTCH THE JUDGE
BARS: HUTCH PRO
STEM: HUTCH DEEP H
HEADSET: TANGE MX125
CRANKS: HUTCH AEROSPEED
SPROCKET: HUTCH AEROSPEED WITH TAKAGI CHAINRING
PEDALS: HUTCH PRO BEARTRAP
CHAIN: IZUMI
HUBS: HUTCH
RIMS: ARAYA 7X
TYRES: MITSUBOSHI COMP IV
SEAT: KASHIMAX AERO
SEAT POST: HUTCH
SEAT POST CLAMP: HUTCH DONUT
BRAKE: DIA-COMPE MX1000
LEVER: DIA-COMPE TECH 3
GRIPS: HUTCH
EXTRAS: HUTCH 2N1 HEADSET LOCK, HUTCH PAD SET, HUTCH RAD KAPS

1985

WOODY ITSON'S GOLD HUTCH TRICK STAR

SUBMITTED BY **WOODY ITSON**

If any one bike in the history of BMX could be considered legendary, this is it: Woody Itson's gold-plated Hutch Trick Star. Freestyle rider Itson rode for Hutch and, in 1984, he designed the Trick Star with the manufacturer. There was a Woody Itson signature edition, which would forever link the bike to the rider. This signature edition came with a pink frame, modified forks, pink Z-rims, Woody Itson freestyle bars, pink A'ME grips and Woody Itson 'race lace' hubs devised specially by Brian Scura at Speed Scura Tech (SST).

Itson was given this gold-plated version of his signature Trick Star early in 1986 by Richard 'Hutch' Hutchins as a thank you. Itson had recently turned down an offer to ride for rival manufacturer Diamond Back.

Only a few years later, Hutch ran into money problems and Itson ended up going to Diamond Back anyway. 'In 1987, after Hutch filed for bankruptcy, I gave my gold Trick Star away to a good friend of mine, Jeff Rugg,' says Itson. 'A few years ago I asked Jeff if he still had it, he said yes. I offered to buy it back and he just gave it to me. I spent about a year searching for a few special parts, cleaning, polishing and re-plating parts. This bike is about 90% original. I had to get new tyres, grips, brake cables, brake levers and pedal cages. Everything else is as it was in 1986.'

Interestingly, if Itson hadn't given the bike to his friend in the late 1980s, he probably wouldn't own it today. He explains: 'When I went to college I put everything I owned in a storage shed apart from one frame and fork and everything got stolen. If this bike had been in there I would have lost it for ever. I'm really glad I did what I did because I got it back and now I have it for my kids to enjoy.'

Hutch parts include the frame, forks, stem, seat, seat post clamp, cranks, pedals, tyres and Woody Itson bars. Other components include SST Woody Itson coaster rear hub, SST second generation front hub, ACS graphite Z-rims, A'ME Unitron grips and SST Command post.

Woody Itson signature 'race lace' coaster brake hub, made by SST. 'A race lace pattern is where all the spokes pull from the outside of the hub inwards – so it makes for a more structurally rigid wheel,' explains Itson. 'But the problem is when you race lace a regular old coaster brake – it will tear the flanges off because it puts so much torque on them. So Brian [Scura] at SST figured out a way to make the race lace pattern into an aluminium shell. So he designed the shell and he had a regular coaster hub press fitted in so he could build me really strong wheels. These wheels were nylons, yet with this set up they were almost as stiff as alloy wheels, because of the spokes and the way it would tighten up. These hubs were very limited production and something very specific to freestyle.'

A RESTORATION PROJECT HUTCH TRICK STAR

SUBMITTED BY **SCOTT REKDAL**

In the last few years restoring old-school 1980s BMX bikes has become really popular – particularly as guys that used to ride back in the 1980s now want their kids to have the same kind of BMX fun that they did 20 or 30 years ago. BMX rider Scott Rekdal from Virginia took some shots of his rusting pink Hutch Trick Star that his parents originally gave him for Christmas back in 1986, but which has been rusting away in his shed for years. With the help of specialist bike-restoration company C4 Labs, Scott restored the bike and took another series of shots. Here we reveal how Rekdal's old rust-bucket was transformed to as-new condition...

C4 Labs (based in Delaware, USA) restored Rekdal's bike. The frame, forks, seat post, seat post clamp, bars, pedals, brake calipers and handles were chemically stripped and powdercoated the original Hollywood Hutch Pink colour.

The sprocket underwent the same process but in crisp white.

The cranks, stem, headset and ACS rotor were cleaned and polished to make them as new.

'In the early 1980s, I bought my first "real" BMX bike,' recalls Scott Rekdal, who recently restored his 1986 pink Hutch Trick Star. 'It was a beautiful chrome and black Hutch Pro Raider. I put tons of cash into it to get it race-ready. I raced it for one season until it got stolen from my backyard. Needless to say I was crushed.

'My parents asked me about what my dream bike would be. Much to their surprise, I told them a pink Hutch Trick Star freestyle bike. It was the most exotic, pro bike I could think of. Secretly, my parents started putting money away for the Trick Star and my dad worked a second job to help pay for it by Christmas. I'll never forget walking down the stairs [on] Christmas morning in 1986 to see the bike of my dreams sitting right there in my living room.

'Fast forward to 2009. I dug the old rusted Trick Star from the shed in the backyard. I found Chip Bowers at C4 Labs Custom Powdercoating online who restored my Trick Star back to how it looked that Christmas morning in '86. Here it is.'

The original saddle was replaced with a new-old-stock part. The restored bike features new A'ME grips, decals, brake cables, chain and brand-new white Skyway Tuff II wheels with new tyres. C4 Labs also made the custom Trick Star stand.

1985
CW CALIFORNIA FREESTYLER

SUBMITTED BY **JUAN MATTOS**

Mike Buff was on CW's trick team in the mid 1980s and assisted with the redesign of the manufacturer's California Freestyle bike. In 1985, a previously designed 'luggage rack' version of the bike was recalled and a limited number of 500 of the improved 'Buff' version were released to CW dealers with serial numbers ranging from BUFF001 (Buff's own frame set) up to BUFF500. The bike pictured here is Mike Buff's original frame, identifiable because of its serial number, BUFF001.

FRAME: SKYWAY STREET BEAT
FORKS: SKYWAY STREET BEAT
BARS: MK 1 SKYWAY EZ
STEM: ACS ROTOR
HEADSET: TIOGA BEARTRAP 2
CRANKS: SUGINO CT 175
SPROCKET: TIOGA CD
PEDALS: ODYSSEY LIMITED EDITION JIM CIELENCKI PEDALS (GLOW GREEN IN THE DARK)
WHEELS: SKYWAY TUFF II
TYRES: HARO FREESTYLE
SEAT: ELINA LIGHTNING BOLT
SEAT POST: TIOGA LAIDBACK
SEAT POST CLAMP: HUTCH DONUT
BRAKES: FREESTYLE 980
LEVERS: STAR MX
GRIPS: A'ME ROUND
EXTRAS: DICE VALVE CAPS

1985
SKYWAY STREET BEAT

SUBMITTED BY **GAVIN LUCAS**

Skyway introduced the Street Beat, its first dedicated freestyle frame, in late 1985, selling frame and fork sets in either white, green or orange. Skyway also did an exclusive deal with CW, who produced lavender, green, orange, pink and more brightly coloured Tuff II wheels specially for the manufacturer. This made for some brightly coloured bikes.

This particular green 1985 Street Beat is actually the bike responsible for this book. Its owner, one of the authors, built it almost entirely from NOS or survivor parts in 2004 after finding a decal-free frame and fork set unmade in a warehouse in the United States for sale online. Once built, the conversations it started proved catalytic for the undertaking of the *Rad Rides* book project.

1988
SKYWAY STREET BEAT

SUBMITTED BY **CHRIS HILTON**

Skyway also brought out another Street Beat in 1986 but the 1988 version is recognizable by its part-chrome, part-paint finish. The Street Beat bike had actually been completely redesigned from the front fork through to the rear dropouts, with the most notable change being that the chromed standing platform and the back end of the creased top tube was knurled, giving it a rough, grippy surface – all the better for standing on.

Sold originally as a complete bike in three different colourways (black, aqua (shown) or red), the 1988 Street Beat was loaded with top-quality parts, including Dia-Compe brakes with Tech 7 locking levers, Tioga Task Force cranks, Suntour freewheel, Haro Freestyle tyres and A'ME grips. Plus a host of Skyway parts like the then brand-new Turbo Disc chainwheel, Skyway Grabber seat and Skyway Spinmaster rotor.

This particular bike in the aqua/chrome colourway was built from a frame and fork set by graphic designer Chris Hilton in London, UK, to exacting standards. It features a few parts not on the original 1988 production bike's spec list: mushroom grips, Skyway axle extenders and Skyway pedals. The choice of white-walled black tyres is a nice touch.

FRAME: SKYWAY STREET BEAT MK II
FORKS: SKYWAY STREET BEAT MK II
BARS: SKYWAY EZ2
STEM: PROFILE
HEADSET: TANGE UNIQUE X
CRANKS: SUGINO 180MM
SPROCKET: SKYWAY TURBO DISC
PEDALS: SKYWAY
CHAIN: KMC 'Z'
WHEELS: SKYWAY TUFF II
TYRES: KENDA COMP III WHITEWALL
SEAT: SKYWAY FREESTYLE GRABBER
SEAT POST: PEREGRINE LAIDBACK
SEAT POST CLAMP: TIOGA SC-5QR (QUICK RELEASE)
BRAKES: DIA-COMPE FS880/AD990
LEVERS: DIA-COMPE TECH 5
GRIPS: MUSHROOM STU THOMSEN SIGNATURE

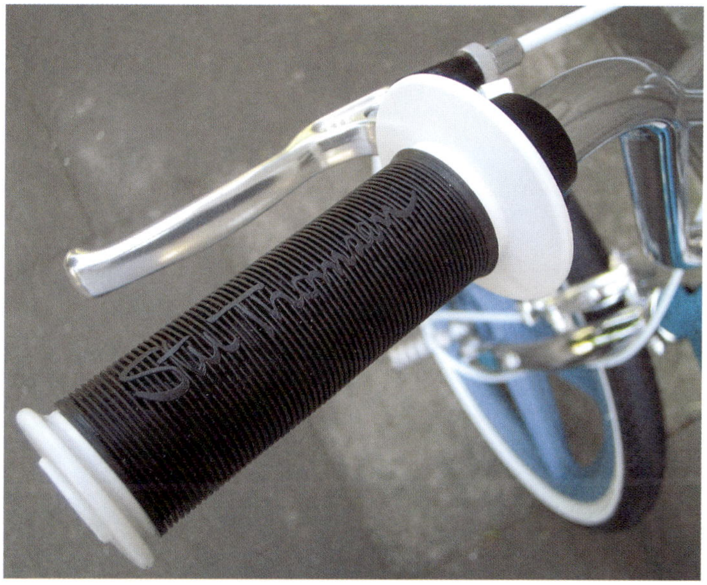

1988
HUTCH XL 24

SUBMITTED BY **JUAN MATTOS**

This gleaming example of a Hutch XL 24 cruiser was submitted by Miami-based collector Juan Mattos, who acquired it from John DeBruin, the current owner of the Hutch Hi-Performance BMX company.

DeBruin has long built show-quality old-school bikes. This particular bike was the show winner at the annual Illinois BMX Show in 2007. He now plans to introduce re-issue bike models, with at least one feature different to the original. 'Using today's technology, I am confident that quality will either meet or exceed the high-quality standards of the originals,' he said in a press release announcing his ownership of the Hutch brand in 2008. 'I will not do anything to jeopardize or degrade the reputation of Hutch as being the finest-quality bicycle components manufacturer ever.'

DeBruin holds the XL 24 bike in particularly high regard: 'I have always thought the XL 24 to be one of the best riding and best geometry frames ever made.'

1988

HARO TEAM SPORT

SUBMITTED BY **DEAN DRUCE**

Australian BMX collector Dean Druce meticulously put together this 1988 Haro Team Sport exactly as it appeared in Haro's 1988 catalogue. A few of the parts are new old stock (NOS), though many are original parts that have been stripped and re-chromed or resprayed. 'It took three years to track down the original white slick tyres,' says Druce. 'Twenty-one years later and I finally have my two dream bikes, Team Sport and Team Master. Just like back in 1988, I can only look at them!'

FRAME: HARO TEAM SPORT
FORKS: HARO
BARS: HARO KNEESAVER
STEM: HARO TEAM
HEADSET: YST
CRANKS: PEREGRINE
SPROCKET: CUSTOM HARO TEAM 44T
PEDALS: VICTOR 555
CHAIN: KMC
HUBS: PEREGRINE SEALED
RIMS: PEREGRINE
TYRES: HARO HP 20 X 2.0
SEAT: VISCOUNT DOMINATOR
SEAT POST: HARO
SEAT POST CLAMP: PEREGRINE
BRAKES: FRONT: DIA-COMPE 883 NIPPON; REAR: DIA-COMPE AD990
LEVERS: DIA-COMPE TECH 77
GRIPS: A'ME
EXTRAS: ODYSSEY GYRO AND CABLES

FRAME: ROBINSON PRO TEAM 19.5"
FORKS: ROBINSON PRO
BARS: ROBINSON PRO
STEM: DK PRO XXL
HEADSET: TIOGA BEARTRAP II
CRANKS: GT POWER SERIES
SPROCKET: GT POWER DISC WITH 44T CHAIN RING
PEDALS: SR MTP
CHAIN: KMC
HUBS: GT SEALED
RIMS: SUN RHYNO LITE
TYRES: TIOGA COMP III 20 X 1.75
SEAT: ROBINSON
SEAT POST: ROBINSON LAID BACK
SEAT POST CLAMP: GT
BRAKES: DIA-COMPE MX-901
LEVERS: DIA-COMPE MX
GRIPS: A'ME TRI
EXTRAS: DT SPOKES

1989
ROBINSON PRO

SUBMITTED BY **DUANE FRANKLIN**

Robinson Racing was established in 1978 by Chuck Robinson, who had originally started out in BMX as the team manager for Webco, before moving on to the DG company where he garnered a reputation for success.

Robinson Racing quickly established itself in the early 1980s as a company that understood race bikes, building a few classic frames, of which the Robinson Pro is one. In 1987 Robinson Racing was sold to the ever-growing power house that was GT.

Chuck Robinson sadly passed away in the 1990s, and with this ended an era of one of the great names of BMX.

'Greg Hill came into my shop and saw my '89 Robinson hanging on the wall', says Duane Franklin, the owner of this particular bike. 'Greg won the NBL National #1 Pro title for '88 on a Robinson, and ran that plate throughout the '89 season on a Robinson. He thought the plate would look good on the bike so he sent it to me. I then changed a lot of the parts so they matched what he would've run at the time. It's not exact, but it's close.'

1989
HARO TEAM MASTER

SUBMITTED BY **DEAN DRUCE**

FRAME: HARO TEAM MASTER
FORKS: HARO
BARS: HARO KNEESAVER
STEM: FUSION
CRANKS: FUSION WITH CUSTOM DECALS
SPROCKET: CUSTOM HARO TEAM 44T
PEDALS: FUSION
CHAIN: KMC
HUBS: PEREGRINE SEALED
RIMS: PEREGRINE
TYRES: HARO MULTISURFACE HPM 20 X 2.0
SEAT: FUSION
SEAT POST: FUSION
SEAT POST CLAMP: FUSION
BRAKES: DIA-COMPE 883 NIPPON
LEVERS: TECH 77
GRIPS: A'ME
EXTRAS: ODYSSEY GYRO WITH CUSTOM-MADE CABLES

Dean Druce also lovingly restored his 1989 Haro Team Master to look just as it did in a press advert from its year of release. The frame design is pretty unique with its 'bashguard' protecting the chainring. When the bike was sold, it came equipped with Haro-designed Fusion components including three-piece alloy cranks, Twintorc seat post clamp, reinforced RXL seat post and a DK-built precision-machined and polished stem.

'This is pretty much how it looked when I opened the box back in '89,' recalls Druce, who had to order it specially as it was never issued in his native Australia. 'Luckily "Scottish" John Buultjens reproduced the decals meticulously,' says Druce. 'That's definitely the centrepiece of the bike. I also had to make the blue gyro cables myself.'

1990s

1990s

By the time the 1990s came around, BMX was facing a serious downturn. The last few years of the 1980s saw BMX sales diminishing, event prize funds shrinking, companies folding and factories closing. BMX faced its biggest challenge to date. It needed some new spice to kick-start what had, up till then, only ever been an industry on an upward curve.

Enter Mat Hoffman. Just as Scot Breithaupt in the 1970s and Bob Haro in the 1980s had flown the flag for BMX before him, Hoffman can be seen as a vital, pivotal figure in BMX in the 1990s. Riding for Skyway and then Haro in the late 1980s as a teenager, Hoffman constantly sought to break boundaries and push the limits of what was possible on a BMX bike. In fact, he is credited with inventing the majority of today's vert tricks. In 1991, aged 20, he set up Hoffman Promotions and his own bike company, Hoffman Bikes. In the same year he also set up the Hoffman Sports Association (HSA), which is still the leading events organization in freestyle BMX. Over the years it has organized such events as the Bicycle Stunt Series, the Crazy Freakin' Bikers (CFB) Series, Soul Bowl and all of the BMX events at ESPN's annual X Games. In 1996, in an exhibition called *Sport As Art*, Hoffman even brought BMX to the closing ceremony of the Olympic Games in Atlanta, Georgia.

The bikes in this chapter of *Rad Rides* are noticeably different from those of the previous decade. Gone were the mag wheels and the crazy Z-rims that might (if you're lucky) bounce back into shape after you bend them. Gone too were the pastel colours and two-tone bikes of the mid 1980s. Also gone, for the most part, were the head-to-toe professional rider uniforms sporting dozens of sponsor logos. In some ways BMX had become too corporate towards the end of the 1980s, with logo-covered riders performing tricks to earn their sponsors money at ticketed events. Riders like Ron Wilkerson of 2-Hip, as well as Mat Hoffman, started to organize their own events that weren't so much about selling BMX products as pushing pro riders' skills to the absolute limit. Meanwhile, kids in car parks or their back yards, dressed in shorts and T-shirts, were dedicating their free time to creating new tricks and riding their bikes in a way that was beyond the understanding of most of the established brand sponsors. These new emerging styles of riding, as it turned out, were also beyond the capabilities of the bikes they were regularly trashing. The bikes just weren't up to hard, experimental street and vert riding.

This is why many BMX bikes in the 1990s looked different to those of the previous decade – they were built differently. Tubing became much wider and thicker (and consequently frames got a lot heavier), which reflected the significant development in how people were riding the bikes. The emphasis had shifted away from racing and flatland – which had become its own distinct discipline by the end of the 1980s – towards big air vert, heavy street and flowing dirt riding. The bikes now had to be built to take a beating, because that's what they would regularly get.

Perhaps it was the fact that the bigger, more established companies such as Haro had more bills to pay and more mouths to feed in the early 1990s that enabled smaller, new BMX companies such as Hoffman Bikes, Wilkerson's 2-Hip, Chris Moeller's S&M Bikes and Rick Moliterno's Standard Byke Company to flourish. Perhaps it was simply that hungry, young inventive riders knew what they needed so just went ahead and designed the bikes they wanted to ride – just as Breithaupt had done in the 1970s and Haro in the 1980s. Whatever the reason, well-crafted, quality frames, invariably manufactured and distributed by new, small, rider-owned companies, hit the streets once again – this time without the hard sell of the (by now) more corporate brands that had blown up and sold out in the boom of the 1980s. BMX was being reborn and rebuilt from the ground up.

And up was the word. Mat Hoffman took BMX to dizzying new heights in the 1990s, literally. In 1993, he was the first person to ride an oversized, specially built 7.3-metre (24-foot) quarter pipe with which he attempted a record-breaking 'high air' by being towed by a motorcycle to gain the speed needed to mount the ramp. In one of his runs he slammed so hard on the way down that he tore his spleen – an accident which nearly killed him. Despite picking up countless injuries and broken bones, Hoffman's exploits on a BMX got the sport the attention it deserved.

Hoffman's HSA was crucial in working with US broadcaster ESPN to create the first X Games event in Providence, Rhode Island, in 1995. 198,000 spectators watched athletes compete in nine different 'extreme' sports including (of course) various BMX events. Despite ESPN's initial plan to stage the X Games every other year, the success of the first event meant that it was immediately established as an annual competition. In the X Games, BMX had gained a new, well-organized, international, televised contest that would spawn new tricks and feats of daring. BMX was back in business.

The 1990s brought to the fore hugely talented riders, including Dave Osato, the late Colin Winkleman, Simon Tabron, Taj Mihelich, Mike Escamilla, Kevin Jones, Day Smith, Dave Morales, Jamie Bestwick and a brilliant vert and street rider sponsored by Haro called Dave Mirra. Such was his talent that Mirra's name is now synonymous with the X Games as, at the time of writing, he has won medals every single year he has competed since the games' inception in 1995. In 2000 he was the first rider to ever perform a double back flip on a BMX in competition.

There is no doubt that the 1990s saw freestyle BMX evolve and diversify way beyond the trick riding that started it all in the early 1980s. The bikes of the period were stronger than ever before. Rick Moliterno's Standard Byke Company even offered lifetime guarantees for all its frames and forks. Vert and trails bikes such as the Hoffman Condor (see page 96) and S&M's Dirt Bike (see page 100) promised indestructibility. Bikes such as the Standard 125 Motocross (see page 107) were designed for race track speed. And bikes like the KHE Premium Lagger (see page 108) were specifically designed for flatland riding. DK bought out the street-specific S.O.B., which stood for slightly overbuilt (see page 119). While BMX might, to some, have looked like a shrinking industry at the end of the previous decade, the 1990s saw strong foundations laid all over the world – foundations that would enable it to keep growing and gaining credibility long into the new millennium.

THE EMPHASIS HAD SHIFTED AWAY FROM RACING AND ALSO FLATLAND – WHICH HAD BECOME ITS OWN DISTINCT DISCIPLINE BY THE END OF THE 1980S – TOWARDS BIG AIR VERT, HEAVY STREET AND FLOWING DIRT RIDING. THE BIKES NOW HAD TO BE BUILT TO TAKE A BEATING, BECAUSE THAT'S WHAT THEY WOULD REGULARLY GET.

Mat Hoffman competing in the vert category of the X Games in 1997.

HOFFMAN BIKES
MADE IN THE U.S.A.
HOFFMAN BIKES "SCUD" BARS
100% 4130 CRMO
HOFFMAN BIKES "MICKEY" POST
OVERSIZED, 1 INCH CRMO
HOFFMAN BIKES T-SHIRT
100% COTTON
CONDOR MODEL - BLUE WITH GREEN STICKERS. COMPETITION READY FOR THE MOST ABUSIVE RIDER. RAMP, STREET, FLATLAND AND TRACK CERTIFIED.
CONDOR MODEL - CHROME WITH RED STICKERS. COMPETITION READY FOR THE MOST ABUSIVE RIDER. RAMP, STREET, FLATLAND AND TRACK CERTIFIED.
words by tim 'broken wrist' ruck
photos by mark 'broken foot' noble
Southsea King Of Concrete was, again, undeniably THE event to attend over all others. It has it all: riding, vert, flat, street, jumping, partying, fighting . . . I'll come to that later. The thing that makes Southsea so special is the emphasis on riding - every terrain is available, it's a measly £5 for which you get 20 hours' use of the park, all of which is usable except for a couple hours per area when the classes are run. You can enter or not for the entry fee [the choice is yours] It's not a 'clinical comp' where you bring your bike, and ride the allotted times, or you don't bring your bike and spectate - you've got the run of the place.
K.O.C.
RIDER
R.I.P
RIDE IN PEACE
KING OF CONCRETE
36 RIDE BMX MAGAZINE
RIDE BMX MAGAZINE 37
dig
£1.50 ISSUE NUMBER
HE SUM OF THE PARTS EQUALS THE WHOLE
GT
RE
SEARCH
SEARCH
SEARCH
SEARCH
SEARCH
SEARCH
93 S&M DIRT BIKE
REDLINE RL540
backyard sucks

Disclaimer
All the products you see are constructed of the finest materials 100% chromoly (even the video's) tested to be the strongest frames on the market... no shit.
TANDARD STUNT CYCLES
. The '92 line up for Standard Bykes translates into a deluge of power. We g power for the duration and can play a wicked short game (flatland). The " and the "Lengthy" will lead the "freestyle" pack in a new direction, the ection. Both bikes feature 100% chromoly construction and each frame and given a personal quality inspection that is, "Right On." Thanks Rydor. Dia- AD 990 stopping. Front roller cam unit for no slippage, oversized tubes and thickness) for sturdy handling and no flex when you kick the nitrous. rse compatible with all Standard Products.
RIDE
BMX MAGAZINE
vert
son airlines test, hoffman
craig reynolds
more king of dirt,
and other crazy bmx stuff
HOFFMAN
Condor
WORDS AND PHOTOS BY MARK NOBLE
WHEN YOUR NAME IS MATT HOFFMAN
RIDE
BMX MAGAZINE
CARLO GRIGGS
europe's top vert rider speaks out
also inside: the chance to win a gt vertigo complete bike; interviews with dylan clayton, jamie bestwick and bart de jong; the big mad hastings jam-o-rama; the wilkerson airlines riot, redline 240, gt vertigo, and ghp pro are put to the test; several not-too-hard-but-good street how-to's; the eba national at slough; all the news from around the world; new products; insane colour poster, new stunt sequences (body varial – peacy buys the farm (slams hard, that is!)
June/July 1993
£1.60
BOBBY FISHER
STANDARD
BYKE COMPANY
PREMIER ISSUE
FREESTYLIN'
GO
THE RIDER'S MANUAL
HIP-HOP, HARLEYS, & HOW-TO'S
RIDE
BMX MAGAZINE
BALLISTIC
HOFFMAN BIKES
SCHOOL'S OUT!! SPECIAL SUMMER FUN ISSUE!
BMX PLUS!
11 FREE BIKES INSIDE!
JULY 1992
MX MUG WINS RACER OF THE YEAR... NOT!
INCREDIBLE BIKE STUNTS
PLUS... FREESTYLE'S DIRTY DOZEN!
WHO WON? SCHWINN vs. HARO vs. MONGOOSE vs. ROBINSON vs.

1992
HOFFMAN CONDOR

SUBMITTED BY **ADAM DAWSON**

Hoffman Bikes was started in 1991 by 20-year-old Mat Hoffman. The company produced some of the finest bikes of the past 20 years, as well as supporting a host of riders, including Dave Mirra, Jay Miron, Kevin Robinson, Chad Kagy, Seth Kimbrough, Taj Mihelich, Brad Simms, Anthony Napolitan, Mike Escamilla, Rick Thorne, Kevin Jones, Chase Gouin, Day Smith, Art Thomason and many more. Hoffman bikes can lay claim to being responsible, in a large part, for the revolution of BMX.

To do justice to Hoffman's influence on the scene we'd need to write another book, however, the Condor and his maverick company have given everything to progressing the sport. The list of now-classic Hoffmans includes the Big Daddy, the Condor, the Flash, the Taj, the Evel Knievel... It's a list that could go on and on.

The bike shown here is a 1992 Condor, named after Hoffman's nickname 'The Condor', for his tuck no-hander – his trademark trick. The Condor bike went through a few iterations in its lifetime, but always represented the greatest strength possible. It was the bike Hoffman rode competitively and it was also his daily ride.

FRAME: HOFFMAN CONDOR
FORKS: HOFFMAN CONDOR
BARS: HOFFMAN PATRIOT
STEM: TNT FREESTYLE INVERTED
HEADSET: TIOGA MX-2
CRANK: GT POWER SERIES THREE-PIECE
SPROCKET: HOFFMAN 45T
PEDALS: HARO FUSION DX
CHAIN: KMC
HUBS: PEREGRINE SUPERPRO 48S
RIMS: PEREGRINE SUPERPRO 48S
TYRES: PRIMO V-MONSTERS
SEAT: ODYSSEY Z77
SEAT POST: HOFFMAN MIKI
SEAT POST CLAMP: INTERGRATED
BRAKES: FRONT: GENERIC SIDE PULL; BACK: DIA-COMPE 990
LEVERS: DIA-COMPE TECH-77
GRIPS: ODI TOADSTOOLS
EXTRAS: HOFFMAN GACK PEGS, ONE OF TWO PROTOTYPE HOFFMAN GRIND DISK BUILT BY TEAM RIDER/DESIGNER CHAD HERRINGTON

FRAME: HOFFMAN BIG DADDY
FORKS: HOFFMAN SUPERFORK
BARS: HOFFMAN LOVE HANDLES
STEM: HOFFMAN
CRANKS: GT POWER SERIES
SPROCKET: HOFFMAN
PEDALS: VICTOR 555
CHAIN: KMC
HUBS: PEREGRINE SEALED
RIMS: PEREGRINE
TYRES: HARO 2.0 WHITE WALLS
SEAT: HOFFMAN
SEAT POST: HOFFMAN
SEAT POST CLAMP: HOFFMAN
BRAKES: FRONT: DIA-COMPE 883 NIPPON; REAR: DIA-COMPE AD990
LEVERS: DIA-COMPE TECH 77
GRIPS: A'ME
EXTRAS: ODYSSEY GYRO

1994

HOFFMAN BIG DADDY

SUBMITTED BY **DEAN DRUCE**

The Big Daddy frame set was designed by flatland pioneer Kevin Jones. The main aim of this frame was to be a flatland frame but, unlike many other flatland-specific frames, the Big Daddy was not limited purely to this discipline. Its short length did, however, make it an incredibly controllable bike and the seat stays (which create a platform around the seat post) were a real bonus for flatland tricks. Strong gussets and a thick down tube guaranteed the Big Daddy to be pretty much unbreakable.

Australian collector Dean Druce, ex-rider and now a civil engineer, has built several bikes, many of which are Haros. 'After spending 18 months getting my 88 Haro Team Master to spec (see page 89) I wanted to do something a little easier,' he says. 'So here it is, my custom SE-made Hoffman Big Daddy in pearl white. The frame is from the original first production run and was made by SE Racing with no serial number. My mate had it rusting in his shed so I restored her.'

1995
STANDARD SHORTY

SUBMITTED BY **DANIEL HARRIS**

The Standard Byke Company was formed in 1991 by ex-Haro rider Rick Moliterno, Krt Schmidt and Bill Nitschke – although Nitschke left the company in 1992. Straight away Standard started designing bikes that were stronger than other bikes on the market at the time. Schmidt told *Th' Link Magazine* in June 2008: 'The bikes we were riding [in the late 1980s and early 1990s] were falling apart every month. During that time biking was going through a transition that added "street riding" to the mix. Riding street was all about discovery and all that innovation was a lot harder on bikes than ever before. Riders wanted to take riding in new directions, but the frames and parts were limiting creativity.'

In 1992 Standard introduced the Lengthy and the Shorty frames. Both had thicker dropouts and were designed to be stronger than other bikes. They also introduced much longer, thicker and stronger pegs than previously seen. Standard was so sure of the strength of its wares that its 1993 catalogue guaranteed all Standard STA, Shorty and Lengthy frames and freestyle forks for life. 'No matter what happens, even if you case a 30-foot set of doubles or get run over by a car, we will fix or replace it free of cost. Not only that, but even if you sell your frame the new owner retains the same lifetime warranty.'

Shown here is a 1995 Standard Shorty, chrome, 1-inch version, which owner Daniel Harris found in a shop a good 15 years after it was made. Harris has lovingly rebuilt it 'as it should have been', he tells us. Note the Peregrine 95-spoke wheels, Primo V Monster tyres, GT three-piece cranks, Standard six-piece bars, Standard forks and S&M stem.

FRAME: STANDARD BYKE SHORTY, 1" VERSION
FORKS: STANDARD BYKE
BARS: STANDARD BYKE FOUR-PIECE
STEM: GT INVERTED
HEADSET: ODYSSEY
CRANKS: GT THREE-PIECE
SPROCKET: GRAVEYARD
PEDALS: JP PRO, TITANIUM AXLES
CHAIN: KMC
WHEELS: PEREGRINE SUPER PRO HP 95 SPOKE
TYRES: PRIMO V MONSTER SKIN WALL 20 X 1.95
SEAT: GT FREESTYLE
SEAT POST: STANDARD BYKE
SEAT POST CLAMP: TNT
BRAKES: ACS BOA (FRONT)
LEVERS: TECH 77
GRIPS: ODI
EXTRAS: STANDARD BYKE REAR HUB GUARD, STANDARD BYKE BAR-ENDS, KORE FLATLAND PEGS

1995
STANDARD STA 500

SUBMITTED BY **DANIEL HARRIS**

The STA (Stronger Than All) was the first of the modern freestyle frames. At its debut in 1993, the STA was the first freestyle frame to use a threadless fork and stem. This frame was the pioneer in the oversized tubing explosion and the philosophy behind it is maximum strength and long-lasting durability.

Fourteen years after its original release, the STA was 'modernized' by the additions of an integrated headtube, mid bottom bracket, externally butted seat tube and smaller dropouts, while still keeping the original character intact.

This is Daniel Harris' STA 500. Harris recalls: 'A friend of mine found this in an old bike shop a few years ago and it had never been built. It was hanging on my wall for a while, and then I decided it had to be built. The STA is one of the strongest bikes ever built and [it] deserved to be shown. I have over 60 bikes and it's my favourite.'

FRAME: STANDARD BYKE STA
FORKS: STANDARD BYKE
BARS: STANDARD BYKE STRIP
STEM: TNT INVERTED
HEADSET: ODYSSEY
CRANKS: GT THREE-PIECE
SPROCKET: REDLINE
PEDALS: JP PRO WITH TITANIUM AXLES
CHAIN: STANDARD BYKE
HUBS: PEREGRINE 48 HOLE
RIMS: PEREGRINE SUPER PRO HPS 48S
TYRES: PRIMO V MONSTER SKIN WALL 20 X 1.95
SEAT: GT FREESTYLE
SEAT POST: STANDARD BYKE
SEAT POST CLAMP: GT
BRAKES: FRONT: ROB RIDGE MEGA (SEALED); REAR: DIA-COMPE ADJUSTER WITH FLEX PLATE
LEVERS: TECH 77
GRIPS: ODI
EXTRAS: PROFILE HOP-UP KIT

1995
S&M DIRT BIKE

SUBMITTED BY **MARK NOBLE**

FRAME: S&M DIRT BIKE
BARS: XPOSURE
STEM: GUSSET CLAMP-ON
CRANKS: REDLINE FLIGHT 401 SERIES, 180MM
PEDALS: SHIMANO DX
WHEELS: SKYWAY TUFF II GRAPHITE
TYRES: FRONT: DYSSEY; REAR: MAXXIS HOLY ROLLER
SEAT: ELINA LIGHTNING BOLT
SEAT POST: CHROMOLY
BRAKE: DIA-COMPE U-BRAKE
GRIPS: JIVE

S&M were formed in 1987 by Greg Swingrover and Chris Moeller. Since then the company has grown to stand for the highest quality available in BMX. S&M's bikes have never left anything to chance. From the Holmes (see page 102), the Dirt Bike and the Sabbath (see page 118) all the way up to the present-day XLAF (see page 131), its bikes have always been strong, simple and made to last, representing excellent value for money. The S&M team history also reads like a who's who of BMX.

S&M parts are, and have been for the past 20 years, some of the best and most reliable parts you can buy. The original Slam bars are still the bars of choice for many riders (in their current incarnation as Slam XLTs), as is the Redneck stem and the Pitch Fork.

The bike shown here is an S&M Dirt Bike. It does exactly what it says on the label – it is built light and strong enough, with a relaxed geometry, to smoothly flow over dirt jumps.

'Ian [Morris] was moving on to a new bike,' explains the owner of this particular Dirt Bike, Mark Noble. 'It might have been when he switched from S&M to ride for Menstrual Cycles [which was under the S&M umbrella anyway, and remains to this day one of the best bike company names ever], and he was kind enough to give me his old frame. Good times.'

1996
TNT HWA FONG DADDY

SUBMITTED BY **BRENDAN GREEN**

TNT is an all-American company that wasn't afraid to experiment when it came to building dirt-jumping frames.

The HWA Fong Daddy, so named for reasons one can only guess at, originally came out in 1995. With a unique double front triangle strength was assured, and the race bike geometry flowed exceptionally well over trails.

In 1997 a Super Fong was also made using T6 aluminium, presumably aimed more at the racer as it was lighter than the HWA Fong Daddy. The rear end of both bikes gave a nod to the designs of the looptail PK Ripper, and with the option of being able to spec the bike with Landing Gear forks, TNT seemed to be respectfully acknowledging two classic pieces of SE Racing's design legacy.

1996
SCHAUFF FLATLAND PROTOTYPE

SUBMITTED BY **JAN SCHAUFF**

Schauff, named after its founder Hans Schauff, is a German bicycle manufacturer that has been making a wide range of bikes since 1932.

This particular flatland BMX was made as a one-of-a-kind prototype for the 1996 BMX Worlds freestyle competition in Cologne, Germany. The single-tube chromoly frame was designed to create as much space as possible for flatland tricks, and the bike used forward-thinking components, such as 1⅛-inch head parts and a cantilever front brake. Unfortunately, it seems most BMX riders at the time weren't quite ready for this radical frame design, so it never made it on to the production line.

1996
S&M HOLMES

SUBMITTED BY **JOSEPH STEVENSON**

FRAME: S&M HOLMES WITH 1" HEAD TUBE
FORKS: S&M PITCHFORK
BARS: S&M SLAM
STEM: S&M REDNECK SHAFTED WITH WEDGIE
HEADSET: TIOGA BEARTRAP
CRANKS: PROFILE
SPROCKET: PROFILE WHIPPET
PEDALS: S&M
CHAIN: KMC
HUBS: PROFILE
RIMS: ARAYA SUPER 7X
TYRES: PRIMO DIRTMONSTER TANWALL
SEAT: S&M LARGE LOGO
SEAT POST: PRIMO ROD
SEAT POST CLAMP: PROFILE
BRAKE: DIA-COMPE AD 990
LEVER: TECH 77 WITH PUSH LOCK
GRIPS: JIVE
EXTRAS: S&M PAD SET

Named after legendary porn actor John Holmes, the S&M Holmes is a race frame with longer proportions than its predecessor, the Dirt Bike. There were three versions of the Holmes with 1-inch headtubes: the Mk1, which was the same as the Mk1 Dirt Bike with thin seat and chainstay tubing; the Mk2, which had loop-like seat stays; and the Mk3, which was the same as the Mk2 Dirt Bike with thicker seat and chainstay tubing. Shown here is the Mk3.

Alex Leech, one of the UK's ex-S&M team riders (and owner of a magnificent collection of S&M bikes), offered Joseph Stevenson this near-NOS Holmes frame that had been under his bed for years. According to Stevenson: 'It had only been built once so was in very fine fettle, and the build came together beautifully. I really enjoyed building this bike, and riding it even more so. The NOS shafted Redneck stem and S&M seat were hideously expensive, but so worth it looking back.'

1997
STANDARD TRAIL BOSS

SUBMITTED BY **DANIEL HARRIS**

FRAME: STANDARD BYKE TRAIL BOSS
FORKS: STANDARD BYKE PRE BASH
BARS: S&M SLAM BARS
STEM: STANDARD BYKE FRONT LOAD
HEADSET: STANDARD BYKE TITANIUM CUPS WITH TANK INTERNALS
CRANKS: REDLINE FLIGHT
SPROCKET: PROFILE WHIPPET
PEDALS: SHIMANO DX
CHAIN: KMC
WHEELS: PEREGRINE SUPER PROS HPS 48S
TYRES: COMP III (2.125 FRONT, 1.75 REAR)
SEAT: ODYSSEY RACE
SEAT POST: ODYSSEY SEMI-LAYBACK
SEAT POST CLAMP: ODYSSEY
BRAKE: DIA-COMPE REAR ADJUSTER WITH FLEX PLATE
LEVER: TECH 77
GRIPS: ODI
EXTRAS: STANDARD BYKE REAR WHEEL ADJUSTERS, STANDARD BYKE TITANIUM HEAD CUPS WITH TANK INTERNALS, KING FRONT AXLE KIT

Robbie Morales has been on the world BMX scene for the last two decades. After proving himself as one of the world's fastest amateur BMX racers, he soon became recognized as one of the world's premier trail riders. He has been part of and has put together some legendary BMX teams, and has used his knowledge to make himself an integral part of some of BMX's most prominent rider-owned companies.

The Trail Boss was, and always will be, associated with Robbie Morales. The bike, his signature model, featured a frame designed by both Morales and Standard's Rick Moliterno utilizing the front end of an STA (see page 99) and the rear end of a Standard 125 Motocross race frame (see page 107). Combining the two created a lighter ride than the STA, but a stronger bike than the 125 Motocross. This bike served as the original blueprint for the first T1, the Progression.

Daniel Harris submitted this bike from his huge Standard collection, and it is a stunning example of a very collectable item. 'The Trail Boss was only built for two years, and it's part of the Standard 250 family. A new version of the bike is being made again today at Standard Byke Company [as is a new version of the STA]. The Trail Boss was designed to be ridden hard and it's stood the test of time. It's now an iconic '90s frame.'

1997
DK GENERAL LEE

SUBMITTED BY **GARY SANSOM**

The DK BMX company (DK stands for Dads and Kids), was founded in Ohio, USA, by Charlie Danishek in 1979 and first came to prominence after releasing the now legendary square-edged DK stem in 1981. It wasn't until the mid 1990s that DK ventured into frame building, with chromoly designs built for both racing and dirt jumping.

In fact, it was this dual purpose that inspired DK to name the General Lee after the car from classic television show *Dukes of Hazzard*. In the programme, the car is constantly speeding or jumping – very fitting for DK's frame concept.

The bike shown here is owned by Gary Sansom, founder of the BMX Museum archive website. Sansom originally started the BMX Museum as an attempt to capture and categorize every BMX bike ever made, and the site now holds close to 50,000 bikes.

'The General Lee is a great example of a theme bike,' says Sansom, 'and the rebel attitude seems to fit BMX very well too. As a child I recall watching *Dukes of Hazzard* every Friday night and loved to see them jump their car.'

1998
HOFFMAN EVEL KNIEVEL

SUBMITTED BY **GARY SANSOM**

FRAME: HOFFMAN EVEL KNIEVEL
FORKS: HOFFMAN EVEL KNIEVEL
BARS: HOFFMAN EVEL KNIEVEL
STEM: HOFFMAN
CRANKS: PROFILE 180MM
PEDALS: ODYSSEY TWISTED
WHEELS: HOFFMAN HIGH ROLLER WHEELSET WITH 48 SPOKES AND SEALED HUBS
TYRES: HOFFMAN
SEAT: HARO DAVE MIRRA
SEAT POST: HOFFMAN
BRAKE: DIA-COMPE 990
LEVER: DIA-COMPE 990
GRIPS: JIVE
EXTRAS: PROFILE BOTTOM BRACKET, ODYSSEY GYRO

The Hoffman Evel Knievel tribute bike launched in 1998 in a run of 500. Motorbike daredevil Knievel was a huge influence on Hoffman, and the two struck up a relationship after their first meeting in person. The bike, loosely based on an oversized Condor, was built the way Knievel would have wanted a BMX to be built: big and strong.

'The Hoffman Evel Knievel bike came from Mat Hoffman's love of Knievel as a child,' explains Gary Sansom. 'He had planned to do one bike per year for each major jump, but ended up making only two. It did allow him to meet and talk with his childhood hero. I believe it was one of the heaviest production bikes ever, and has become quite a collectors' item.'

1998
STANDARD TAO

SUBMITTED BY **JOSH SMITH/JOE ALDER**

FRAME: STANDARD TAO
FORKS: STANDARD 1 1/8 RACE, MODIFIED BY STANDARD (990 MOUNTS WELDED ONTO THE FORKS)
BARS: STANDARD CUSTOM-MADE FOUR-PIECE BULLIT
STEM: ODYSSEY FLATWARE
HEADSET: DIA-COMPE SST
CRANKS: PROFILE 175MM
SPROCKET: PROFILE IMPERIAL, 28T
PEDALS: KHE STIMULATOR7
CHAIN: SHADOW CONSPIRACY INTERLOCK 2
HUBS: FRONT: PROPER; REAR: SUNTOUR COASTER, MODIFIED BY SUNTOUR WITH FLANGE, COG AND ARM WELDED, 12T KORE COG ADDED TO THE COASTER, WELDED COASTER BRAKE BRACKET MOUNT
RIMS: ODYSSEY RIB CAGE
TYRES: REVENGE PINNER 1.95
SEAT: ODYSSEY 99ER
SEAT POST: ODYSSEY INTAC
SEAT POST CLAMP: HOFFMAN
BRAKES: DIA-TECH HOMBRES
LEVERS: DIA-COMPE TECH 77
GRIPS: ANIMAL EDWIN (WITH FLANGES CUT OFF)
EXTRAS: EASTERN BAR-ENDS, SNAFU DUAL TOP GYRO CABLE, ODYSSEY SLICS GYRO CABLES (THE TAO USES A DUAL CABLE ROUTE, SO REGULAR ODYSSEY GYRO CABLES ARE NOT USED), ODYSSEY SLIC FRONT BRAKE CABLE, ODYSSEY G3 GYRO (GYRO TOP PLATE CUT TO WORK WITH THE FLATWARE STEM), S&M GYRO TABS (TAPPED HEADTUBE TO ACCOMMODATE BOLT ON AND SLITS CUT INTO THE SIDES FOR EASIER CABLE REMOVAL), HOFFMAN DAY SMITH LOC'ED PEGS

The Tao is a flatland frame designed in 1996 by Paul Osicka (a flatland rider for Standard at the time). With religious and philosophical connotations, the Chinese word *Tao* means 'way' or 'path', and is intrinsically linked to the concepts of Ying and Yang – the symbol for which Standard referenced in its graphics for the bike. According to Osicka, the design of the frame is a simplistic liberation from the unnecessary gimmicks of other flatland rides. With a very unusual head gusset, the Tao featured a 19-inch top tube with a 74.5 degree headtube, and 13.25-inch chainstay. Importantly, it also had no platform.

After first having his Tao painted neon green by Standard, Josh Smith, the owner of this ride, decided to sell the bike in favour of a Quamen (see page 132). In 2009, after becoming friends with prolific Standard BMX collector Daniel Harris, Smith was reminded of his old 'green machine'. 'That's when I decided to look online and see if anyone had a Tao for sale,' he explains. 'When I looked at the search results I couldn't believe what I was seeing; a Tao, in neon green – I had found my old Tao! I contacted the seller straight away, and it was home within a week.'

As the frame was a little worse for wear, Smith sent it back to Standard for a new paint job. Standard also repaired the frame, fixing a few dents, and welded a coaster bracket to the chainstay. 'When building the frame up I made some additional modifications of my own,' he says, 'including something I had seen Rick Moliterno do; I had the coaster brake cog welded to the driver so it wouldn't come loose. I did the same with the coaster arm, and had it welded to the nut.'

Josh Smith has since parted company with his beloved Tao for a second time. Why did he get rid of it again? He decided to give it to one of his flatland heroes Joe Alder (who, together with brothers Jeremy and James, was known as one of the Alder brothers).

'Back in the '90s, a lot of guys were loving Kevin Jones' riding, but I discovered another guy named Joe Alder. One day, while looking through Facebook, I found Joe and sent him a friend request. From there we actually became good friends and I asked him if he was still riding. I was shocked to find he still had his old Team Master (the bike he rode in the Alder Tricks 2 video), and I decided right there and then that I was going to get the "green machine" Tao fixed and built up to give to Joe. We set up a date to meet in York [Pennsylvania], for the annual York Jam, and I presented Joe with the Tao. He was blown away. I hope he's been getting to ride it lately.'

1998

STANDARD 125 MOTOCROSS

SUBMITTED BY **JOSEPH STEVENSON**

FRAME: STANDARD 125 MOTOCROSS
FORKS: STANDARD BASH
BARS: STANDARD 2PC STRIPS
STEM: S&M REDNECK XLT
HEADSET: CHRIS KING
CRANKS: PROFILE
SPROCKET: STANDARD 36T
PEDALS: ODYSSEY
CHAIN: KMC
HUBS: FRONT: CHRIS KING; REAR: ODYSSEY TRACK MARK
RIMS: FRONT: PRIMO; REAR: SUN RHYNO LITE
TYRES: ODYSSEY TRACK MARK
SEAT: FIT ECCD
SEAT POST: THOMSON
SEAT POST CLAMP: S&M XLT
BRAKE: AD999
LEVER: ODYSSEY TRIGGER
GRIPS: ODI SUBLIMINAL
EXTRAS: XLITE TITANIUM BOLT BAR-ENDS, ONZA CHILL PILL HANGER, STANDARD PAD SET, UGP NUMBER PLATE

The original Standard 125 was the first BMX race frame to incorporate a threadless fork and stem combination, as well as pioneering the use of high-tech air-hardened tubing. 'This is by far and away my favourite build,' explains the bike's owner Joseph Stevenson. 'In my opinion [this is] one of the greatest BMX frames ever built – how many modern bikes were inspired by the Standard 125?'

Stevenson came across a complete set of Standard 125 Motocross stickers on eBay, and then set out on the hunt for a frame. 'I wanted a good frame, so paid through the nose to get this one shipped from the States. I then started sourcing red components, as I had planned the powdercoat colour to be postbox red. But when the frame came back from being painted it was darker than originally intended, and the red components just clashed. I then stuck the whole thing in my loft in disillusionment, and forgot about it for ages,' says Stevenson.

Later, when sorting through spares, Stevenson happened to hang a few polished parts on the frame and then the bit was back between his teeth. 'I'd already built several era-correct bikes so decided to have a break and threw the era book out of the window. I built this bike entirely for me. I spent hours polishing the parts for this build – the attention I paid to the detail made me laugh at myself.'

1998 MONGOOSE DMC

SUBMITTED BY **CHRIS WILLET**

One of the pioneers of freestyle BMX in the 1980s, Dennis McCoy remains a true competitor in the sport to this day. He has been at the top of competitive BMX freestyle for over 25 years, participating in a combination of street, vert, flatland and dirt contests. He holds the longest winning streak in freestyle competition history, claiming a BMX year-end title every season from 1986–1995 – a decade of domination. To highlight the longevity of McCoy's career, he pulled a 900 in the vert category at the very first X games in 1995, and he pulled another in the final of the X Games in 2009, aged 42.

In addition to his long list of riding credits, McCoy is also the head of McCoy Productions, which he runs with his wife Paridy. The couple help organize BMX contests and events, including the Dew Tour, and McCoy also works as a TV analyst for NBC and ESPN.

The 4130 chromoly-made DMC was created as a signature bike for McCoy, who began riding exclusively for Mongoose in the early 1990s. It was first released in 1995, and featured chromoly tubing with specially designed handlebars, wheels and tyres. The DMC was created for use by serious freestyle riders and came with a suggested retail price of US$725.

FRAME: MONGOOSE DMC
FORKS: ODYSSEY 41 THERMAL
BARS: FISHBONE SUSHI
STEM: SNAFU BAR
HEADSET: FSA DH PRO SEALED
CRANKS: PRIMO POWERBITE
SPROCKET: PRIMO 36T
PEDALS: PRIMO TENDERISER MAGNESIUM
CHAIN: GUSSET SLINK
HUBS: GSPORT 9/16" HOMER
RIMS: ALEX SUPRA E
TYRES: HARO MULTISURFACE 3 WHITE WALLS
SEAT: FISHBONE BIGBONE
SEAT POST: FISHBONE BIGBONE
SEAT POST CLAMP: SNAFU HEXAGON
BRAKES: ODYSSEY EVOLVER
LEVERS: DIA-COMPE TECH 77
GRIPS: ODI LONGNECK
EXTRAS: PRIMO SEALED BOTTOM BRACKET, ODI DONUTS, SNAFU BAR-ENDS, ODYSSEY G3 GYRO AND CABLES, ODYSSEY SLIC CABLE, BARADINE BRAKE PADS, PRIMO 14G SPOKES, PRIMO NIPPLES, ODYSSEY 13T FREEWHEEL, FISHBONE TURNPEGS

1999 KHE PREMIUM LAGGER

SUBMITTED BY **MATTHEW COWLE**

KHE was founded in 1988 by German brothers Thomas (a keen freestyle rider) and Wolfgang Goring. The company name refers to their home city, Karlsruhe, which is often abbreviated to K'he. The company's first products in the early 1990s were parts – pegs, a solid chainwheel called the KHE Grinddisc, forks, and a seat post clamp. The Premium Lagger frame, the company's second after its 1993 Catweasle, was designed by US BMX rider Jesse Puente specifically for flatland riding. At the time it was first released in 1996, it changed the way flatland bikes looked and were designed for ever. Its geometry was tailored specifically for the kind of riding Puente had made a name for himself by perfecting since the late 1980s.

FRAME: KHE PREMIUM LAGGER
FORKS: ODYSSEY CS2 FLATLAND ZERO RAKE
BARS: KHE SWISS MISS
CRANKS: STOLEN MOB THREE-PIECE
SPROCKET: STOLEN MOOD
PEDALS: DIAMOND BACK
HUBS: FRONT: STOLEN ROULETTE, REAR: KHE REVERSE FREECOASTER
RIMS: ALEX SUPRA G
TYRES: CHENG SHING WHITE WALLS
SEAT: STOLEN P BOSS PIVOTAL
SEAT POST: STOLEN CHOKER
EXTRAS: DIAMOND BACK PEGS, SNAFU MOBEUS GYRO, FLY BIKES GYRO PLATE, STOLEN WHIP FRONT CABLE

1999
TERRIBLE ONE PROGRESSION

SUBMITTED BY **NATHAN VAN DRIEL**

FRAME: T1 PROGRESSION
FORKS: MOSH BRASS
BARS: 1664
STEM: MOSH
HEADSET: FSA
CRANKS: PROFILE RACING
SPROCKET: MACNEIL 39T
PEDALS: ODYSSEY JIM C/DK PLASTIC
CHAIN: KMC 410
HUBS: MOSH FRONT, 1664 REAR
RIMS: ALEX MX22
TYRES: PRIMO
SEAT: NORCO
SEAT POST: MOSH
SEAT POST CLAMP: MOSH
BRAKE: DIA-COMPE 990
LEVER: TEKTRO
GRIPS: ODYSSEY DUALLY

In 1998 Robbie Morales left Standard Byke Company to start a new outfit with legendary pals Joe Rich and Taj Mihelich. Mihelich (previously of Hoffman Bikes) was one of the all-time great dirt jumpers, and the link-up with Morales seemed like a promising one. Rich brought his street riding expertise to the new firm and Terrible One (T1) was born.

The Progression was Morales' signature frame. The geometry and build were similar to that of the Standard Trail Boss (see page 103) and it was an easy and relaxed frame to ride.

There were only two versions of the Progression made: the first without a wishbone, and the second with. The wishbone forms a stronger join between the chainstays and the bottom bracket. However, it adds more weight and might be thought to give a less rigid ride. Morales' time with T1 was short, lasting only a couple of years before he left to start up Fit Bikes. His departure was due to manufacturing difficulties and the inability to meet the growing demand for the Progression frame.

'My Progression started off as a gloss red, first batch, 20-inch top tube frame,' explains Nathan Van Driel. 'One of approximately 250 frames made from the first batch, it has survived relatively unscathed, save for a few minor dings on the down tube and dropouts. It's recently been repainted gloss white, and I still have the original "Made in New York" sticker from the day it came off the welder's bench around 1999.

'I've actually had the opportunity to talk to Robbie Morales twice, and after mentioning that I was still using his signature frame eight years after it had finished production, he got a big smile on his face. It's a testament to the quality of welding done by the frame builders at Spooky Cycles in New York that it's withstood the spills and crashes of years and years of [riding] skate parks and city streets.'

1999
S&M NEXT GENERATION HOLMES

SUBMITTED BY **JOSEPH STEVENSON**

FRAME: S&M NEXT GENERATION HOLMES
FORKS: S&M PITCH
BARS: S&M BUTLER
STEM: S&M REDNECK
HEADSET: DIATECH/ PRIMO GORILLA
CRANKS: DEMOLITION SPINE
SPROCKET: KINK
PEDALS: S&M
CHAIN: KMC
HUBS: SEVENTIES
RIMS: ALEX SUPRA
TYRES: PRIMO WALL
SEAT: ODYSSEY TEAM
SEAT POST: PRIMO
SEAT POST CLAMP: PRIMO VIKING
BRAKE: SHIMANO XT DEORE
LEVER: TECH 77
GRIPS: ODI LONGNECK
EXTRAS: ODYSSEY BAR-ENDS, PRIMO PEGS

In an attempt to keep up with the trends of the day, it could be said that S&M actually ruined the Holmes when they made the Next Generation (NG), as it was so overbuilt. When most people think of S&M's heavy 1990s frames, it's usually the Sabbath or Warpig frames that come to mind, and the NG Holmes often gets overlooked.

'I've always had a secret liking for the NG Holmes,' explains Joseph Stevenson, 'as I rode one back in the late '90s. Then a few years ago someone offered me this frame at a silly price, and I happened to have a rare set of original Holmes Big Cock decals for it. The frame was originally clear-coated, but, being named after the porn star John Holmes, the only colour I could really restore it to was white. As with a lot of mid-school parts everything else on the bike was low-priced and easy to come by at the time.'

1999
S&M CHALLENGER

SUBMITTED BY **JOSEPH STEVENSON**

FRAME: S&M CHALLENGER 21" TT AD MOUNTS 1-1/8" HEADTUBE
FORKS: S&M RACE FORK
BARS: S&M SLAM BARS
STEM: S&M REDNECK
HEADSET: SOLID NEEDLE BEARING
CRANKS: PROFILE
SPROCKET: PROFILE WHIPPIT
PEDALS: S&M
CHAIN: KMX Z
HUBS: GT SEALED
RIMS: ARAYA SUPER 7X
TYRES: PRIMO DIRTMONSTERS
SEAT: S&M BIG SHIELD
SEAT POST: S&M RAMROD
SEAT POST CLAMP: PRIMO
BRAKE: DIA-COMPE AD 990
LEVER: TECH 77
GRIPS: ODI LONGNECK

Built for speed (in both 20- and 24-inch versions), the S&M Challenger's name references the space shuttle that blew up disastrously in 1986. In addition to the frame and forks, the Challenger product line also consisted of handlebars and a stem, all of which were originally released in 1993.

'This was my first proper mid-school restoration,' explains Joseph Stevenson. 'The frame came as a rusty hulk and was sat in my workshop for years. I'd been picking up nice mid-school stuff and stashing it away since the late '90s so had most of the parts to hand. I then happened on a set of Challenger stickers on eBay and snagged them for peanuts.'

Keeping to the colour scheme of the S&M shield, the thinking behind the build was a do-it-all bike, something that could be used at the trails, but that could still handle a lap of the local race track.

2000s AND BEYOND

2000s AND BEYOND

A lot has happened in the last ten years of BMX. Throughout the 1990s and the 'dead' years of BMX, things went back to basics and, although it was a tough time for BMX, it meant that riders got better and the bikes got better too. The heavy, overbuilt bikes of the 1990s have gradually been replaced with a new breed of pared-down, lightweight and technologically advanced rides.

Bikes have also become more specialized, with subtle tweaks distinguishing a park or trails bike from a street bike. For instance, trail bikes are usually solidly built with two-piece handlebars and no front brake; street bikes often don't have any brakes at all, with pegs for grinds and four-piece handlebars; park bikes usually have a back brake and a gyro for bar spins; flatland bikes usually feature straight-laced spokes, pegs and a smaller pinion; and race bikes tend to be very lightweight with only a back brake and have smooth tyres to benefit from the new style of tarmac-heavy race tracks.

Technical advances have seen materials pushed to their limits, with aluminium, titanium and even carbon fibre being tried and tested in everything from frame design to the smallest nut or bolt. Just look at Joe Stevenson's Eastern Grim Reaper (see page 134) that uses a titanium frame with areas cut out for maximum weight reduction, or Ken Spaulding's Terrible One SFA (see page 128) with custom-made parts utilizing aluminium and titanium to achieve the ultimate specification. Today's race bikes also boast an array of technological advances, and it's unusual to see one without an alloy frame and carbon fibre forks. That said, manufacturers such as Supercross are even pushing the limits of what can be achieved with chromoly, claiming that some of their products are actually lighter than their carbon fibre equivalents.

It's not just the materials that are evolving either, innovations such as internal headsets, external bottom brackets and cassette hubs have all made their appearance on bikes in recent years. Much of today's race bike innovation actually comes from the world of mountain biking. VSI Products, a manufacturer founded and run by BMX legend Toby Henderson, has taken this one step further. VSI's Speed brand is a race BMX concept which uses an integrated frame, fork and wheel system (or 'rolling chassis'). This includes specially designed front and rear hubs that use larger 20mm hollow aluminium axles, combined with massive 32mm hub/dropout interfaces on the frame and forks. Taking a cue from MTB technology, this new rolling chassis is noticeably stiffer, resulting in greater power transfer for faster gate starts and more precise handling. To find out more check out race pro Nick Koehler's team bike on page 143.

One other mountain bike-related change to race BMX bikes has seen the controversial use of Shimano Pedaling Dynamics (SPD) clip pedals, rather than traditional platform pedals. Although they first appeared in the 1990s, clips only started to become the norm in the early 2000s. They deliver more power to the rider, as well as giving greater control when jumping, pumping and manualing. The flip side to this is that if riders start to use clips too early, they tend to end up as less-skilled riders. There is also the question of safety, as pro racer Bubba Harris found out in 2007 when he dislocated his ankle in a time trial at the official Olympic race track in Beijing, China.

It would be impossible to write the introduction to this chapter without mentioning the fact that in 2003 the International Olympic Committee made BMX a full medal Olympic sport for the 2008 Olympic Games in Beijing, China. This was a truly momentous event for BMX – what started out as a group of kids emulating their motocross heroes in a disused field had now become a global sport watched by millions of people around the world. Latvian Maris Štrombergs and Anne-Caroline Chausson of France were crowned the first male and female Olympic champions respectively.

Despite the high of becoming an Olympic sport, it could be said that BMX racing wasn't actually that popular until the action sports competition X Games introduced a Downhill BMX category in 2000. One thing is for certain: X Games certainly raised the profile and popularity of BMX in general, and particularly for the freestyle aspect of the sport.

Set up by US sports broadcaster ESPN, X Games is a televised annual action sports event where participants compete to win bronze, silver and gold medals, plus prize money. Over the years the competition has given birth to many first-time tricks, such as Tony Hawk's 900 in skateboarding, Anthony Napolitan's double front flip on a BMX, and Travis Pastrana's double back flip in freestyle motocross. Just as importantly, the games helped money flow back into BMX, meaning that riders were getting paid enough to dedicate themselves to the sport full-time.

If there is one name that has become synonymous with X Games over the years, it is without question that of Dave Mirra, the record holder for most X Games medals in any sport. Mirra has won medals in every X Games since they began back in 1995 and, in 2008, he was even placed second in the BMX Big Air category and third in Rally Car racing. Known primarily as a vert ramp and park rider, Mirra had been sponsored by Haro since the mid 1990s before starting his own bike company, Mirraco, in 2006.

An interesting development in Mirra's career saw him as the star of the *Dave Mirra Freestyle BMX* video game released in 2000. Featuring Mirra and a selection of other professional riders, the aim of the game was to ride through a total of 12 different levels, completing objectives and unlocking new equipment on the way. The game was certainly relevant to Mirra, and he was once quoted as having said he was 'throwing tricks you would only think possible in a video game', while talking about his vert riding style.

The relationship between Mirra and his on-screen representation puts forward an interesting question: where does the evolution of BMX stop? As the technology improves and because riders' imaginations are never-ending, the mentality is: if you can do it in a computer game, then you can do it in real life. Riders today are at a level that kids back in the 1970s never thought possible, even in their wildest dreams. 360-degree tail whips, double back flips, front flips… The list goes on. It seems the sky really is the limit when it comes to BMX.

Throughout the last decade the resurgence of BMX has been astounding. The revival that Mat Hoffman started in the 1990s has snowballed and BMX has now firmly re-established itself as a permanent part of global culture. One thing's for sure – BMX is certainly no fad.

IT WOULD BE IMPOSSIBLE TO WRITE THE INTRODUCTION TO THIS CHAPTER WITHOUT MENTIONING THE FACT THAT IN 2003 THE INTERNATIONAL OLYMPIC COMMITTEE MADE BMX A FULL MEDAL OLYMPIC SPORT FOR THE 2008 OLYMPIC GAMES IN BEIJING, CHINA.

Dave Mirra riding his infamous 24k gold-plated bike during the BMX Freestyle park final at the 2005 X Games. Mirra went on to take first place, despite previously suffering a concussion in the vert event.

BMX
A TOPE!

Nº 12 Otoño 2009 5€

ZONA FREE
ESPECIAL
FERIA FESTIBIKE

ENTREVISTA
CRISTIAN
BECERINE

CAMPEONATO DE EUROPA
DINAMARCA

FINAL CTO. ESPAÑA
PADUL

CAMPEONATO DEL MUNDO 2009
AUSTRALIA

Just Plain Fast
MARIANA PAJON
GOLD, ELITE WOMEN

macneil
DILLON LLOYD

GERMANOPEN 08
MONDLANDUNG IN IZHEVSK
BMX RACE VS. OLYMPIA 2008
BARAK INVITATIONAL
EMPIRE OF DIRT
ON TOUR IN COSTA RICA
WILDAU TRAILS JAM

Masters of
Cream
international bmx lifestyle magazine hors-serie #6 / summer 2008 / free

2000
S&M SABBATH

SUBMITTED BY **JOSEPH STEVENSON**

FRAME: S&M SABBATH
FORKS: S&M PITCHFORK WITH AD MOUNTS
BARS: S&M CASTILLO
STEM: S&M
HEADSET: SOLID NEEDLE BEARING
CRANKS: PRIMO POWERBITE
SPROCKET: 44 INDUSTRIES
PEDALS: S&M
CHAIN: KMC Z
HUBS: FRONT: PRIMO S.O.B.; REAR: CAMACURA
RIMS: FRONT: PRIMO HULA HOOP; REAR: ODYSSEY
TYRES: PRIMO V MONSTER
SEAT: PRIMO STEROID
SEAT POST: S&M RAMROD WITH MARVINS GUTS
SEAT POST CLAMP: PRIMO VIKING
BRAKES: FRONT: DIA-COMPE AD 990F, DIA-COMPE FLEXIE; REAR: DIA-COMPE AD 990 TWIN CABLE, ODYSSEY GYRO, PRIMO PERVERT
LEVERS: TECH 77 WITH ODI BRAKE NECKS
GRIPS: PRIMO LOGO
EXTRAS: PRIMO ALLOY BAR-ENDS, PRIMO X4 PEGS

Designed by BMX rider Sean McKinney and first produced in the late 1990s, the Sabbath was S&M's first attempt at creating a flatland frame. As with most other bikes of the time, it was built with durability in mind, including beefy tubing and a rear end that featured an angled standing platform. The graphics were, of course, inspired by Ozzy Ozbourne's band Black Sabbath, and the bike itself went on to inspire other iconic designs from S&M, including the Troy McMurray-designed Warpig frame.

Redesigned in 2000, the new Sabbath has no platform and, although it's still a flatland frame at heart, plenty of riders use it for street and even vert riding.

The bike shown here was built by Joseph Stevenson, who had set himself the challenge to use as many NOS parts as possible. 'I had the frame originally as a wall flower, as I'd picked it up in brand-new boxed condition. I'd gotten the notion that I wanted to build a really compact but tank-like heavyweight ride, a flat/tech street build, and being a Sabbath it could only be black. I've always loved all-black bikes and had a fondness for the overbuilt 90's bikes, so it was a treat to build, and felt unbreakable to ride.'

2001
FIT BIKE SERIES 1

SUBMITTED BY **MARC SEEMANN**

FRAME: FIT SERIES 1
FORKS: S&M PITCHFORK
BARS: S&M SLAM
STEM: FLY BIKES
HEADSET: SOLID
CRANKS: PROFILE
SPROCKET: FBM
PEDALS: WELGO
CHAIN: KMC
HUBS: FORMULA
RIMS: ALEX
TYRES: ODYSSEY
SEAT: KINK
SEAT POST: PRIMO ROD
SEAT POST CLAMP: DK
BRAKE: DIA-COMPE 990
LEVER: ODYSSEY
GRIPS: ODI LONGNECK

After a stint with Standard, Robbie Morales joined Terrible One (T1) as a team rider and helped create his renowned lightweight trails signature frame, the Progression (see page 109).

Two years after the creation of the Progression, and with only 50 frames made in that time, Morales decided to leave T1 to try to bring his frame to the masses. With the backing of Chris Moeller of S&M, Morales went on to set up Fit Bikes and the Fit Bikes team in 2000, taking the design of the Progression with him under the guise of the Series 1. With manufacturing taken care of by S&M, the Series 1 was clean, simple, light and arguably helped to spark the evolution of better-designed street and park frames. As Marc Seemann, owner of this particular bike, explains: 'To me this bike represents a major turning point in BMX design, it was the first largely popular frame to kick off the modern design of toned down BMX frames.'

Morales eventually split with Moeller and Fit Bikes in 2009 and set up a new BMX company named Cult.

2002
DK S.O.B.

SUBMITTED BY **STEVE MITCHELL**

FRAME: DK S.O.B.
FORKS: DK JUMP
BARS: DK TWO-PIECE CHROMOLY
STEM: DK JUMP
HEADSET: TANGE SEIKI SEALED
CRANKS: DK CHOPSTICKS WITH SEALED BB
SPROCKET: DK IRON CROSS 39T
PEDALS: HARO FUSION
HUBS: FORMULA 14MM SEALED HUBS
RIMS: ALEX DOUBLE WALLS
TYRES: MAXXIS HOLY ROLLER
SEAT: DK JUMP
SEAT POST: DK FIXED
SEAT POST CLAMP: DK TWO-PIECE
BRAKE: DIATECH HOMBRE
LEVER: ODYSSEY MODULEVER
GRIPS: DK IRON CROSS
EXTRAS: ACS FAT CLAW FREEWHEEL 14T

The S.O.B. (slightly overbuilt) was designed to be the strongest freestyle and street frame on the market. Designed by legendary rider Colin Winkleman, the S.O.B. took over a year to develop and was built completely from oversized American cromoly tubing, with a 2-inch down tube and 1-inch chainstays. It also featured a wishbone design on both the top tube and bottom bracket shell for maximum strength.

'2002 is the last year the S.O.B. was made, and the first and only year it was built and sold as a complete,' says Steve Mitchell. 'I bought the bike at a garage sale and rebuilt it to almost original spec. The only thing not original are the wheels, which are Alex rims with Formula hubs. Otherwise it has the original frame, fork, bars, stem, seat clamp, seat post, seat, brakes, cranks and chainring.'

2002

2-HIP BIKES PORK

SUBMITTED BY **DAVE HUDSON**

FRAME: 2-HIP BIKES PORK
FORKS: ODYSSEY FREESTYLE
BARS: HARO FOUR-PIECE KNEESAVERS
STEM: ODYSSEY CHOCK FULL O' NUTS
HEADSET: FSA PIG
CRANKS: FSA SMACK DADDY 175MM
SPROCKET: KINK 33T
PEDALS: PRIMO TENDERIZER
CHAIN: KMC 410HX
HUBS: ODYSSEY HAZARD
RIMS: ODYSSEY HAZARD LITE
TYRES: FRONT: PRIMO TAJ; REAR: HOFFMAN SKIDMARK
SEAT: PRIMO HEMORRHOID
SEAT POST: ODYSSEY INTAC
SEAT POST CLAMP: DK TWO-PIECE
BRAKES: ODYSSEY EVOLVER
LEVERS: ODYSSEY MODULEVERS
GRIPS: S&M
EXTRAS: ODYSSEY GTX-R GYRO, ODYSSEY J-PEG LIGHTS PEGS

2-Hip Bikes was founded in 1993 by Ron Wilkerson, and the company is still making bikes today. The company set out to build 'the strongest frames in BMX' – no mean feat, but their products rarely left riders believing otherwise.

The name 2-Hip was already well-known in BMX as Wilkerson had originally ridden as part of the 2-Hip trick team in the early 1980s and also organized various independent 2-Hip freestyle events in the late 1980s, such as the King of Vert competition.

'I have a deep affection [for] the BMX bikes made during the "overbuilt" period of BMX,' says Dave Hudson. 'The frames and components were built to last and take all the punishment you could throw at them. It was the norm during that time for a rider's bike to be 40lbs [18kg] plus. The Pork is one of my favorite frames as it was the beefiest, and one of the heaviest, frames built. It has a beautifully made front triangle consisting of fat two-inch tubes with the iconic top tube piercing of the headtube. During this era manufacturers strived for their frames to stand out and have a different look from the other competitors. The industry was steeped in creativity; no two frames looked the same and the underlying belief was, "the heavier, the stronger!" For me, the Pork epitomizes the era and best represents a time when riders wanted a bike that would hold up to all the new tricks they were creating. Keeping with that vibe I selected primarily overbuilt, heavy parts that were widely used and respected during the same period. I will have this bike till I die.'

2003
MOSH METHOD

SUBMITTED BY **JURJEN SEMEIJN**

In 1996 Giant Bicycles created its Mosh BMX division with the help of Linn Kastan and AA Pro Jason Richardson. Although Mosh is no more, the brand is still seen to have had a big influence on the BMX industry; partly for choosing riders not just for their ability, but also for their unique style.

The bike on this page was owned by Jurjen Semeijn, an entrepreneur, artist and BMX enthusiast from Amsterdam. 'I have always had nice looking bikes, but this one I liked a lot. I received the frame as a present from Mosh and most of the parts were given to me by friends. The frame is custom-painted in "fifties aqua" and to match the Cadillac theme I wanted most parts in chrome. Special touches were cut down brake lugs, upside-down chromed revolver stem and Chris King headset. The seat was a Mosh sample.'

FRAME: MOSH METHOD
FORKS: ODYSSEY RACER
BARS: MOSH
STEM: REVOLVER
HEADSET: CHRIS KING
CRANKS: SNAFU
SPROCKET: MOSH
PEDALS: SNAFU
HUBS: MOSH
RIMS: SUN BIG CITY
TYRES: MOSH SHADOW
SEAT: MOSH SAMPLE
GRIPS: MOSH
EXTRAS: MOSH BAR-ENDS, MIKE ARDELEAN'S TITANIUM PEGS

2004
Y3 WETHEPEOPLE

SUBMITTED BY **Y3**

FRAME: WETHEPEOPLE
FORKS: WETHEPEOPLE
CRANKS: WETHEPEOPLE
TYRES: ODYSSEY
STEM: WETHEPEOPLE
WHEELS: SKYWAY TUFF II
SPROCKET: WETHEPEOPLE
PEDALS: ODYSSEY
BARS: WETHEPEOPLE

Founded in the very early 1990s by BMX riders Stephan Prantl, Stefan Rose and Lars Dorsch in Cologne, Germany, wethepeople started out designing and distributing limited edition T-shirts for German BMXers. It was only towards the end of that decade that the company started to create high-end, rider-designed BMX bike parts and products, releasing its Everlast handlebars in 1999. Frames designed for different forms of freestyle riding followed in 2003 and now wethepeople's stable of sponsored freestyle riders hail from all over the world.

The Y3 BMX bike was the result of a 2004 collaboration between German BMX company wethepeople and adidas' fashion brand Y3 (itself a collaboration between adidas and Japanese designer Yohji Yamamoto).

The Y3 Autumn/Winter 2004 collection paid homage to youth and street culture from the twentieth century and the bike was produced to accompany and promote the collection. The bike sported orange Skyway Tuff II wheels and was shipped with assembly instructions that even the least technically minded follower of fashion would be able to follow. It also came with a designer price tag: US$2,520. Only 50 were made.

2004
BROOKLYN MACHINE WORKS POOKY CRUISER

SUBMITTED BY **JOE AVEDESIAN**

Brooklyn Machine Works (BMW) was founded in 1996 by Joseph Avedesian and partners, who began making components for their bikes together, as they kept breaking the parts they were using. They soon found themselves making parts for friends, and demand for their talents quickly blossomed. Today, BMW has grown into an iconic bike manufacturer renowned for making premium-quality products from its workshop in New York. In recent years its profile received a further boost when rapper, singer, record producer, composer and fashion designer Pharrell Williams became a co-owner of the company.

The Pooky Cruiser, aka the TT Cruiser (short for twin top tube), evolved from the 1996 Brooklyn Cruiser, and was updated to use 135mm rear disc hubs with a milled-aluminium disc brake hanger and chain tensioner. The Pooky was available as a set including frame, forks and matching stem, or as a 'special order' complete bike.

FRAME: SUPERCROSS EVO 24
FORKS: BOMBSHELL F1 CARBON FIBRE
BARS: MCS RON C CRUISER
STEM: PROFILE ACOUSTIC
HEADSET: CHRIS KING NOTHREADSET
CRANKS: PROFILE
SPROCKET: DK IRON CROSS LITE
PEDALS: PREMIUM SLIM
HUBS: PROFILE MINI CASSETTE
RIMS: VELOCITY TAIPAN DEEP V 24
TYRES: INTENSE MICRO KNOBBLIES
SEAT: S&M SLIM
SEAT POST: THOMSON ELITE LAYBACK
SEAT POST CLAMP: PROFILE SLIM JIM
BRAKE: SHIMANO DEORE
LEVER: ODYSSEY TRIGGER
GRIPS: SHADOW CONSPIRACY ASPHALT
EXTRAS: PROFILE DOG COLLAR BAR-ENDS, ALLOY NIPPLES, ALLOY VALVE CAPS

2005 SUPERCROSS EVO 24

SUBMITTED BY **CHRIS LAW**

Pushing the boundaries of aluminium BMX race-frame technology, Supercross Evo race frames are hand-built using customized Easton ultra-light alloy, making them one of the lightest frames on the market.

The custom Evo cruiser shown here was built by Chris Law, one of the founding members of *Spine* magazine, street-based design firm Unorthodox Styles, and cult sneaker website Crooked Tongues. Law has also worked as a footwear designer at adidas Originals in Portland, Oregon, part of the Addict Clothing design team in London, UK, and now works as a design director for Converse All Star in New York.

Law has a great collection of custom builds. For more details, see our interview with him on page 150. This particular bike has a metallic cola-inspired paint job, accented with metallic root beer, mango and black components. Law's background in sneaker design is certainly evident in his builds, revealing itself through his stylistic use of colour and keen attention to detail.

JIM BAUER'S CUSTOM PROJECTS METAL REBEL CONTENDER

SUBMITTED BY **JIM BAUER**

Started in 1999 by (ex-S&M) BMX pro James 'Jimmy' Levan, Metal Bikes make high-quality 100% chromoly frames, and the Rebel Contender is its lightweight trail and street frame.

All three bikes on this spread are owned by Jim Bauer, the creative director of Odyssey BMX and, as you can see, Bauer has owned some of the most colourful and creative bikes of the last decade. While growing up, Bauer was inspired by the BMX manufacturers (such as Cyclecraft) who used to offer custom paint jobs on their frames, forks and bars, and since then he has always painted his bikes – sometimes as often as every two weeks.

Bauer's role as creative director means he is involved in everything at Odyssey, from team management to product testing. He's also a well-known rider in his own right, pulling off such insane tricks as the infamous Death Gap – jumping a huge gap on the sixth floor of a construction site.

METAL IS MOSTLY ABOUT JIMMY LEVAN AND HIS LIFE. JIMMY WAS A HERO OF MINE GROWING UP, AND I AM GLAD TO CALL HIM ONE OF MY FRIENDS NOW. METAL IS HIS COMPANY AND [IN] EVERY ASPECT [YOU] CAN SEE SOME PART OF HIS PERSONALITY SHOWING THROUGH. JIMMY REALLY IS THE "ROCK AND ROLL" OF BMX. HE DOES WHAT HE WANTS, HOW HE WANTS, AND HE DOESN'T MUCH CARE WHAT HAPPENS. TWIST THE THROTTLE AND HOLD ON. JIMMY IS BMX.
—JIM BAUER

2006

To create this tile design, Bauer started with a mint-green production frame, getting the forks, rims, bars and cranks powdercoated to match. He taped off the grid with masking tape, spray painted over the top, and then hand-painted the grid to eliminate any overspray and clean up the edges.

FRAME: METAL REBEL CONTENDER 21" PROTOTYPE
FORKS: ODYSSEY DIRECTOR
BARS: ODYSSEY CIVILIAN HI
STEM: ODYSSEY ELEMENTARY W/O TABS
HEADSET: FSA SEALED
CRANKS: ODYSSEY TWOMBOLT LHD (175)
SPROCKET: ODYSSEY VERMONT 28T
PEDALS: ODYSSEY JC/PC PROTOTYPE
CHAIN: KMC 710
HUBS: FRONT: ODYSSEY VANDERO; REAR: ODYSSEY LHD CASSETTE WITH HOLLOW AXLE/10T DRIVER
RIMS: GSPORT RIBCAGE 36 HOLE
TYRES: FRONT: ODYSSEY AITKEN 2.25; REAR: ODYSSEY PATH 2.1
SEAT: ODYSSEY SENIOR 2 RAILED
SEAT POST: ODYSSEY 25.4 INTAC
SEAT POST CLAMP: INTEGRATED
GRIPS: ODYSSEY AARON ROSS GRIPS
EXTRAS: GSPORT PLEGS PEGS

2007

This bike started out raw, so the first step for Bauer was to powdercoat the entire kit fluorescent pink. Using lots of lightning bolt die-cut stickers and custom-made logo stickers (Metal, Odyssey, Lavar, Defgrip), Bauer then laid the reverse stencil for the pink. On top of the pink went a dove-grey base coat, followed by a fluorescent yellow-and-green splatter. The die-cut stickers were then removed to let the pink show through, and the entire bike was semi-matt clear-coated.

FRAME: METAL REBEL CONTENDER 21"
FORKS: ODYSSEY DIRECTOR
BARS: ODYSSEY CIVILIAN HI
STEM: ODYSSEY ELEMENTARY V2
HEADSET: FSA SEALED
CRANKS: ODYSSEY TWOMBOLT LHD (175)
SPROCKET: ODYSSEY VERMONT 28T
PEDALS: ODYSSEY JC/PC PROTOTYPE
CHAIN: KMC 710
HUBS: FRONT: ODYSSEY VANDERO; REAR: ODYSSEY LHD CASSETTE REAR (HOLLOW AXLE/10T DRIVER)
RIMS: GSPORT RIBCAGE 36 HOLE
TYRES: FRONT: ODYSSEY AITKEN 2.25; REAR: ODYSSEY PATH 2.1
SEAT: ODYSSEY SENIOR 2 RAILED
SEAT POST: ODYSSEY 25.4 INTAC
SEAT POST CLAMP: INTEGRATED
GRIPS: ODYSSEY AARON ROSS GRIPS
EXTRAS: GSPORT PLEGS PEGS

FRAME: METAL REBEL CONTENDER PROTOTYPE 21"
FORKS: ODYSSEY DIRECTOR
BARS: SUNDAY FORUMPH
STEM: ODYSSEY ELEMENTARY V3
HEADSET: ODYSSEY SEALED INTEGRATED
CRANKS: ODYSSEY TWOMBOLTS LHD (175)
SPROCKET: ODYSSEY VERMONT 28T
PEDALS: JC/PC FINAL PRODUCTION SAMPLES
HUBS: FRONT: GSPORT MARMOSET 36H; REAR: GSPORT RATCHET, 9T, 36H
RIMS: GSPORT ROLLCAGES 36H
TYRES: AITKEN KLYTE 2.25"
SEAT: AITKEN PROTOTYPE
SEAT POST: PROTOTYPE
SEAT POST CLAMP: INTEGRATED
GRIPS: ODYSSEY CHASE HAWK
EXTRAS: ODYSSEY PARENDS BAR-ENDS, GSPORT TAPERHEX NIPPLES, GSPORT PLEGS PEGS

2009

In order to create the lace effect on his 2009 ride (as shown above left), Bauer covered the parts to be spray painted with actual lace – using it as a kind of stencil. After spray painting everything in gold he then masked off 'window' areas before painting everything purple with red accents. The masking tape was then peeled away to reveal the gold lace pattern. 'The rims wouldn't last if I had brakes,' says Bauer.

2007
TERRIBLE ONE SFA

SUBMITTED BY **KEN SPAULDING**

The SFA (which stands for Sweet FA) is the signature frame of Terrible One (T1) team rider Garrett Byrnes. 'I first saw this frame at Interbike in 2007,' says Ken Spaulding, the owner and builder of this particular bike. 'It was the only SFA that I'd seen with a press-fit headtube and, as I am a diehard Chris King supporter the press-fit was a must-have.'

Spaulding asked T1 founder Joe Rich if he was willing to part with the frame, but it was going to be ridden by Byrnes himself. A couple of weeks later, Spaulding heard that Empire BMX shop had another frame that somebody had custom-ordered but never collected. 'I called Empire and placed the order right away,' says Spaulding, 'and I've been on this frame ever since – it's by far my favourite bike that I've ever had.'

Incredibly, most of the parts on this bike were made by Spaulding himself (under his company name Zodiac Engineering); the 27T full-guard sprocket, front hub, stem, seat post, bar-ends and cable hanger were all custom made. Spaulding also modified other components as he saw fit. The crank arms have been narrowed to reduce the Q factor (the distance between the pedal attachment points on the crank arms) and the pedal spindles were shortened to bring the pedals closer to the arms for a more comfortable ride. The forks were also deepened to lower the front end and bottom bracket, and to steepen the headtube angle.

'This is the bike that all of my prototype parts have been tested on and some of them have gone into production. All of the parts on the bike that aren't black were sandblasted, tumbled and then polished. I also chemically etched "ZodiacEng." on the top tube and down tube and "Long live the press-fit" on the headtube.'

FRAME: CUSTOM TERRIBLE ONE SFA 21" TOP TUBE WITH PRESS-FIT HEADTUBE
FORKS: ODYSSEY RACE CLASSIC, STEERER SHORTENED, DROPOUTS DEEPENED BY 3/8"
BARS: TERRIBLE ONE RUBENS
STEM: ZODIACENG., COUNTERBORED FOR FLUSH PRELOAD BOLT, BLUESIX BIKES TITANIUM BOLTS
HEADSET: CHRIS KING 1-1/8" NOTHREADSET
CRANKS: ODYSSEY WOMBOLT 175MM, CAP REMOVED, SPINDLE SHORTENED, HEX RECUT, PRELOAD SHORTENED, Q FACTOR 167MM
SPROCKET: ZODIACENG., 27T, FULLGUARD
PEDALS: ATOMLAB TRAILKING, SPINDLES SHORTENED, BROACHED FOR A 6MM HEX KEY
CHAIN: KMC 710SL, TIN COATED
HUBS: FRONT: ZODIACENG. FULL 7068, F1 CERAMIC, HYBRID CERAMIC BEARINGS, BLUESIX BIKES TITANIUM BOLTS; REAR: CHRIS KING 12T, 36H TITANIUM FEMALE 14MM AXLE, BLUESIX BIKES TITANIUM BOLTS
RIMS: G-SPORT RIB CAGE 36H
TYRES: ANIMAL ASM 2.1"
SEAT: MACNEIL SL PIVOTAL, BLUESIX BIKES TITANIUM BOLT
SEAT POST: ZODIACENG., WEDGED
BRAKE: SUELO, BOTTOMS MILLED FOR CLEARANCE, BLUESIX BIKES TITANIUM BRAKE PAD NUTS
LEVER: PAUL COMP LOVE
GRIPS: DIMENSION TRACK
EXTRAS: ZODIACENG. BAR-ENDS, ODYSSEY (SHORTENED) PRELOAD, KINK LINEAR BRAKE CABLE, ZODIACENG. HANGER WITH STEEL THREAD INSERT AND HEAT-TREATED SET SCREW, DT SWISS 14G SPOKES, DT SWISS NIPPLES, VELCRO LOOP

2007 TERRIBLE ONE CUSTOM PAUL B

SUBMITTED BY **JOSEPH STEVENSON**

Joseph Stevenson managed to acquire this very rare frame after a discussion with Joe Rich from Terrible One (T1). When Stevenson mentioned an interest in the possibility of a custom frame with a long top tube, Rich told him that T1 team rider Paul Buchanan had just built up a new bike and that his old frame was sitting in the store room, surplus to requirements. Stevenson jumped at the chance given the frame's rarity and interesting history. It was custom built by Solid Bikes for Terrible One with a 21.5-inch top tube, and the front end is from a T1 Hickerson Moody frame with the chainstay wishbone from a T1 Ruben frame.

The build itself was inspired by Stevenson's love of opposites; the raw and slightly rusty frame, forks and bars all contrast nicely with the polished alloy components, and Stevenson sourced titanium bolts and spokes which all seemed right for the build. A notable extra is the Onza Chill Pill straddle cable hanger that a jeweller friend of Stevenson's polished and inlaid with mother-of-pearl. 'The bike felt natural and fit me perfectly,' says Stevenson. 'It'll stay with me for life and at present is suspended from the ceiling in my living room.'

FRAME: TERRIBLE ONE CUSTOM PAUL B 21.5"
FORKS: S&M PITCH XLT
BARS: S&M GRAND SLAM
STEM: S&M REDNECK XLT, TITANIUM BOLTS
HEADSET: CAMPY CHORUS/ CARBON SPACER
CRANKS: PROFILE RACE, TITANIUM AXLE, FLUSH AND TIMING BOLTS
SPROCKET: S&M TUFFMAN 30T
PEDALS: S&M 101 SEALED
CHAIN: KMC
HUBS: FRONT: CHRIS KING HUB 36, BLUE6 BOLTS; REAR: PROFILE CASSETTE 36, TITANIUM AXLE, DRIVER AND NUTS
RIMS: FRONT: SUN RHYNO LITE; REAR: SUN BFR
TYRES: KENDA SMALL BLOCK
SEAT: ECLAT
SEAT POST: ECLAT
SEAT POST CLAMP: RNC TITANIUM
BRAKE: DIATECH AD999, TITANIUM BOLTS
LEVER: COLONY
GRIPS: ODI SUBLIMINAL
EXTRAS: ODYSSEY PARENDS BAR-ENDS, HEATSINK BRAKE PADS WITH BLUE6 TITANIUM NUTS, NOKON BRAKE CABLE, TITANIUM SPOKES

FRAME: CUSTOM 21.5" XLAF, CHAINSTAY BRAKES, EXTRA CABLE GUIDE, ENGRAVED HEADTUBE
FORKS: S&M PITCH XLT
BARS: S&M GRAND SLAM
STEM: S&M REDNECK XLT/RACE XLT HYBRID
HEADSET: CAMPAGNOLO
CRANKS: PROFILE
SPROCKET: S&M TUFFMAN
PEDALS: S&M ONE-O-ONE
CHAIN: KMC SUPERLIGHT
HUBS: FRONT: CHRIS KING; REAR: PROFILE
RIMS: FRONT: SUN RHYNO; REAR: BFR
TYRES: PRIMO DIRTMONSTERS
SEAT: S&M
SEAT POST: THOMSON
SEAT POST CLAMP: S&M XLT
BRAKE: FLY
LEVER: ODYSSEY TRIGGER
GRIPS: S&M THIN
EXTRAS: S&M BAR-ENDS

2007
S&M XLAF

SUBMITTED BY **JOSEPH STEVENSON**

This is a fully custom frame, a one-of-a-kind S&M XLAF (Extra Long As Fuck), organized by ex-S&M team riders Alex Leech and Ian Morris. Following Joseph Stevenson's numerous talks with Leech about getting a frame that actually fitted him, a few enquiries were made about building a custom S&M. Stevenson then emailed the geometry to S&M founder Chris Moeller, and two months later the frame arrived. As Stevenson describes: 'It was beautiful, with a long TT, a healthy standover height and near flawless workmanship – this was a bit special, my own custom made S&M.'

2008 QUAMEN CLAD G8

SUBMITTED BY **KEN SPAULDING**

'Back when I started riding I always wanted to ride flatland,' explains this bike's owner Ken Spaulding, 'but I could never afford a proper bike so I just rode my GT Mach 1 with two brakes and four pegs – it was terrible for what I wanted, but it worked.' Fast forward ten years and California-based Spaulding decided to build a proper flatland bike. He contacted local independent BMX company Quamen, who specialize in top-quality frames and parts.

Spaulding paid the company a visit, touring the facility before rounding up the parts to build his bike. His frame of choice was the Clad G8, a chromoly flatland frame designed and perfected by Quamen over the past ten years. Although he originally just wanted the frame, Spaulding ended up leaving with a stem, crank arms and a couple of sprockets too.

As with all of Spaulding's builds, this bike features a few special touches, custom-made by Spaulding himself. He had already turned the hubs from a piece of 7068 aluminium bar stock, lacing them to G-Sport rib cages, and he also made the pegs, dust cap and seat clamp.

FRAME: QUAMEN CLAD G8
FORKS: INERTIA
BARS: LONDON BIKES
STEM: QUAMEN 26MM, COUNTERBORED
HEADSET: ZODIAC DUST CAP, NEEDLE BEARINGS
CRANKS: QUAMEN 165MM, NON-DRIVE SIDE KNUCKLES REMOVED, SPINDLE: BLUESIX 6AL/4V TITANIUM, SHORTENED BY .200", NON-DRIVE SIDE SPACER: ZODIAC 7068
SPROCKET: QUAMEN 18T
PEDALS: STLN THERMALITE
CHAIN: KMC 710SL (NOT SHOWN) TIN COATED
HUBS: FRONT: ZODIACENG., FULL 7068, F1 CERAMIC, HYBRID CERAMIC BEARINGS, BLUESIX BIKES TITANIUM BOLTS, REAR: FEDERAL, 9T, 36H, SC INTERNALS, FEMALED
RIMS: G-SPORT RIBCAGE, 36H
TYRES: TIOGA FS100, ODYSSEY FREQUENCY G
SEAT: KHE WATANABE
SEAT POST: THOMSON ELITE 25.4MM
SEAT POST CLAMP: ZODIAC
GRIPS: DIMENSION TRACK
EXTRAS: STLN PRELOAD WITH TURNED OD AND FACE, QUAMEN STAINLESS BAR-ENDS, DT SWISS 14G SPOKES, DT SWISS NIPPLES, ZODIAC 7068 PEGS

2008
FLY BIKES TIERRA

SUBMITTED BY **KYLE PUCEK**

FRAME: FLY BIKES TIERRA 19.6
FORKS: FLY BIKES TIERRA
BARS: FLY RACING 5.5 ALUMINIUM
STEM: FLY BIKES POTENICA 40MM
HEADSET: EASTERN INTERGRATED
CRANKS: SUELO 160MM
SPROCKET: DRIVE 25T
PEDALS: ODYSSEY TWISTED PC GLOW IN THE DARK
CHAIN: KHE HALF LINK
HUBS: FRONT: STOLEN ROULETTE; REAR: KHE REVERSE FREECOASTER
RIMS: STOLEN ROULETTE GLOW IN THE DARK
TYRES: FLY BIKES CALLGERA FOLDABLE
SEAT/SEAT POST: KHE LOYAL SEAT AND POST COMBO
SEAT POST CLAMP: FLY BIKES
BRAKE: FLY BIKES
LEVER: DIATECH GOLD FINGER
GRIPS: FLY BIKES RUBEN
EXTRAS: JAGWIRE BRAKE CABLE

Spanish BMX company Fly Bikes was set up in 2000 by a group of friends who wanted to realize their dream of creating their own bikes. Fly has a reputation for both an excellent team of riders from all over the world (Spain, Australia, France, Italy and the United States among others), and for innovative products that help shape the modern BMX product landscape.

Available with three different top-tube sizes, the Tierra is Kevin Porter's signature frame and features a low seat stack height (for easier tailwhip-ability) and an offset seat tube with a short back end (giving the feeling of a roomier front end). It's constructed from 100% heat-treated chromoly with an integrated headtube, Spanish BB (a bottom bracket size invented by Fly Bike's David Quesada), and removable cable guides for custom cable routing.

The flat black and toxic green bike (with glow-in-the-dark pedals and rims) shown here was built by Kyle Pucek from Wisconsin, USA. 'The idea behind this build was to create a bike for my 10-year-old son – something unlike any other bike I had seen. Finding components that were light for him was really important, so I used parts such as aluminium race bars as I felt he wouldn't break them.'

2008
EASTERN GRIM REAPER

SUBMITTED BY **JOSEPH STEVENSON**

FRAME: EASTERN TITANIUM GRIM REAPER
FORKS: ODYSSEY RACE
BARS: BERRINGER LITE
STEM: ODYSSEY ELEMENTARY
HEADSET: EASTERN
CRANKS: ODYSSEY WOMBOLT
SPROCKET: ODYSSEY MDS
PEDALS: ODYSSEY TWISTED PC
CHAIN: KMC 710SL TITANIUM NITRIDED
HUBS: FRONT: CHRIS KING 36 HOLE WITH TITANIUM BOLTS; REAR: PROFILE CASSETTE WITH TITANIUM AXLE, TITANIUM DRIVER AND TITANIUM NUTS
RIMS: FRONT: SUN RHYNO LITE; REAR: SUN BFR
TYRES: KHE PARK
SEAT: MACNEIL PIVOTAL WITH KNIGHT TITANIUM BOLT
SEAT POST: MACNEIL CHOPPED
BRAKE: FLY
LEVER: ODYSSEY TRIGGER
GRIPS: ANIMAL EDWIN
EXTRAS: ODYSSEY BAR-ENDS, TITANIUM SPOKES, KHE TWIGGY INNER TUBES

Eastern is known for pushing frame design to the limits with weight-saving cut-outs (just look at the headtube cut-out and slotted seat tube on their Grim Reaper frame, above). Upping the ante even more (some would say at the expense of strength and durability), the titanium Grim Reaper frame weighed in at under 1kg (2lbs).

'This project was something I'd been perusing for a long time,' explains Joseph Stevenson. 'How light can you make a BMX?' To answer this question Stevenson started with the titanium Grim Reaper frame, and the rest was a process of simply checking the weight of components with manufacturers.

'I could have gone further with it, but it seemed pointless at just over 17lbs [7.7kg]! The trouble was I had no confidence in the strength of it – a mental block that it was so light, it just had to be weak. It convinced me that titanium wasn't the best choice for a BMX frame, it's just too flexible.' According to Stevenson the best thing about the bike was watching other people ride it: 'No one could help but crack a smile with how it zipped forward when you cranked it.'

'One thing I will say for the Reaper,' he continues, 'it was genuinely beautifully made. There's a theory that a Soviet fighter plane engineer that goes by the name of "Batch" welded these frames – the fit and finish of the tubes was perfect, all the welds were flawless and every one was ground smooth. I could never keep it as a daily rider though, I just know I'd break it.'

2008
MACNEIL WHITTON

SUBMITTED BY **HARRISON BOYCE**

FRAME: MACNEIL WHITTON II
FORKS: BLAZER 10MM
BARS: S&M XLT
STEM: CELL
HEADSET: FSA IMPACT PRO
CRANKS: MACNEIL CONJOINED 175 WITH TITANIUM SPINDLE
SPROCKET: PRIMARY 25T
PEDALS: F.A.C.E.
CHAIN: KMC 710SL
HUBS: MACNEIL 3/8 FRONT, 14MM 9T BACK
RIMS: ALIENATION
TYRES: ANIMAL GLH KEVLAR
SEAT: SL WOOL BLACK
SEAT POST: STUMP

Canadian BMX company MacNeil was founded in 2000 by pro rider Jay Miron. After riding for Scwhinn for five years, Miron became frustrated with the constraints of a corporate company and decided to go it alone, naming the company with his mother's maiden name.

The Whitton is the signature model of ex-MacNeil team rider Alistair Whitton and special features include an old-school 22.2mm seat post size (rather than the standard 24.5mm of most modern frames).

'This was by far the brightest bike I've ever built up,' says owner of the bike, creative director and rider for MacNeil, Harrison Boyce. 'I get the opportunity to build new bikes on a regular basis and I was planning on only riding this bike for about six months, so I wasn't really worried about going crazy with the colours. Somehow I ended up riding it for over a year and by the time I built up a new bike I was so sick of looking down at the green and orange that I built a completely black bike. Looking back though, this is probably one of my favorite bikes that I've built.'

2008 SUNDAY FUNDAY

SUBMITTED BY **KYLE PUCEK**

Since its inception in 2005, Sunday's priorities have always lain in both aesthetics and design innovation. The Funday is the signature frame of BMX professional Aaron Ross, a rider known for having unique bike set ups, from fluorescent colours to one-off Sunday graphics, and even themed colour schemes such as his 'Watermelon' and 'Orange Soda' bikes. Ross likes to make his bikes stand out, something that becomes obvious when looking through the back catalogue of Funday production bikes.

The owner of the bike shown here, Kyle Pucek, fell in love with the Funday while riding a friend's. 'Then, when the baby blue frame came out (with pink and yellow stickers), it threw me back to my childhood in the 80s when bikes were all neon, and I had to build one. I just went from there and the bike came together really well – the perfect fusion of old style with new products. My favourite part of the bike is the Fly Pantera bars, the V-style just screams old school.'

FRAME: SUNDAY FUNDAY 20.5"
FORKS: SUNDAY MORNING 2.1
BARS: FLY BIKES PANTERA
STEM: FLY BIKES POTENICA 50MM
HEADSET: ODYSSEY INTEGRATED
CRANKS: FLY BIKES 175MM
SPROCKET: FLY BIKES 28T
PEDALS: ODYSSEY TWISTED PC
CHAIN: SHADOW CONSPIRACY HALF LINK
HUBS: FRONT: FLY BIKES; REAR: KHE ASTERN FREECOASTER
RIMS: FLY BIKES
TYRES: EASTERN BIKES BURNOUTS
SEAT: KHE WATANABE
SEAT POST: FLY BIKES
SEAT POST CLAMP: FLY BIKES
BRAKE: FLY BIKES
LEVER: DIATECH GOLD FINGER
GRIPS: PRIMO JOSH STRICKER SIGNATURE
EXTRAS: G-SPORT PLEGS PEGS

2009 FLY BIKES PANTERA

SUBMITTED BY **GEOFFREY JORDAN**

Now in its fourth incarnation, the Fly Bikes Pantera (and Sergio Layos' signature frame) was first released in 2003 and is a classic frame with classic geometry. Features include an integrated headtube, Spanish BB, removable gyro-detangler tabs, chainstay brake mounts and removable chain tensioners.

The bike shown here is a 2009 third-generation frame, which has been built up using almost purely Fly Bikes components by Canada-based Geoffrey Jordan. 'It rides real smooth and I think it looks pretty good too,' he says.

FRAME: FLY BIKES PANTERA 20.8"
FORKS: FLY BIKES PANTERA
BARS: FLY BIKES PANTERA
STEM: FLY BIKES POTENCIA
HEADSET: FLY BIKES
CRANKS: FLY BIKES
SPROCKET: ODYSSEY 28T MDS
PEDALS: FLY BIKES RUBEN
CHAIN: KMC Z510HX
HUBS: FRONT: G-SPORT MARMOSET; REAR: G-SPORT 9T RATCHET
RIMS: FLY BIKES REAR
TYRES: FRONT: FLY BIKES CAMPILLERA 2.25 FOLDING, REAR: FLY BIKES CALLEJERA 2.00 FOLDING
SEAT: FLY BIKES ZUSCO
SEAT POST: FLY BIKES
SEAT POST CLAMP: FLY BIKES
GRIPS: FLY BIKES RUBEN
EXTRAS: FLY BIKES BAR-ENDS, SPANISH FLY BIKES BB, G-SPORT GLANDS HUB GUARD, ODYSSEY JPEG LIGHTER PEGS

2009
FIT BIKE AITKEN 3.5

SUBMITTED BY **DAVE HUDSON**

FRAME: FIT AITKEN 3.5, 20.75"
FORKS: S&M TAPERED-LEG PITCHFORK
BARS: FIT HIGHS
STEM: FIT D.L.T.
CRANKS: PRIMO POWERBITES
SPROCKET: FIT TRI 25T
PEDALS: ODYSSEY TRAIL-MIX
CHAIN: SHADOW V2
HUBS: FRONT: DEMOLITION BULIMIA; REAR: DEMOLITION ANOREXIA CASSETTE HUB 9T
RIMS: ODYSSEY HAZARD LITE
TYRES: FRONT: FIT 2.3"; REAR: FIT 2.1"
SEAT: FIT PIVOTAL
SEAT POST: FIT PIVOTAL
SEAT POST CLAMP: INTEGRATED
GRIPS: FIT DAK
EXTRAS: DT SPOKES, ODYSSEY JPEG LIGHTER PEGS, FBM REAR HUB GUARD

Ex-Mosh team rider Mike Aitken is well known for his style and flow, whether riding street, park or trails. The 3.5 Aitken, one of his signature frames with Fit Bikes, is a lightweight ride with a responsive feel, featuring a teardrop down tube, tapered seat stays and an integrated seat clamp.

'This is our son Seth's main ride,' explains Dave Hudson, who submitted this particular bike. 'It started out when he made a pretty lengthy Christmas wish-list last year. We decided to buy the frame/fork/bars and a few of the other components and get him off to a good start. Then I was online one night and got a great deal on the cranks. One thing led to another and, by the time Christmas was upon us, we pretty much had the whole bike except for a wheelset. Once his grandparents heard of what we were doing they got together and purchased a custom wheelset from Empire BMX. Christmas morning came and, lo and behold, he had a new customized complete bike under the tree waiting for him to assemble. It is a Christmas he will remember forever.'

2009
S&M .38 SPECIAL CRUISER

SUBMITTED BY **ROB ANDERMAN**

The .38 Special 24-inch is S&M's cruiser race bike offering. At home on the trails or in the local park the .38 Special 24-inch is designed for older and taller riders looking for something larger than a 20-inch. A 4130 chromoly tube set makes this a true racing BMX, allowing the rider to feel the ride, while the modern materials and race geometry make for a very light bike that's fast, and quick to respond.

FRAME: S&M .38 SPECIAL CRUISER 21.5"
FORKS: S&M RACE
BARS: S&M RACE 5.75"
STEM: S&M XLT
HEADSET: FSA IMPACT
CRANKS: PROFILE 175MM
SPROCKET: PROFILE IMPERIAL 39T
PEDALS: DMR V12
HUBS: PROFILE RACE 16T
RIMS: SUN RINGLE ENVY
TYRES: INTENSE MICRO KNOBBY KEVLAR
SEAT: KHE DANDY
SEAT POST: THOMPSON ELITE
SEAT POST CLAMP: HOPE
BRAKE: SHIMANO DXR
LEVER: SHIMANO DXR
GRIPS: ODYSSEY AARON ROSS
EXTRAS: WETHEPEOPLE VECTOR BRAKE CABLE

2009
AVENT TR7 CRUISER

SUBMITTED BY **JEREMY HICKS**

Bombshell Inc. and Avent Cycles produce race-proven cycling components to aerospace standards. Hand made at the Avent factory in California, the TR7 claims to be one of the most technically advanced BMX frames on the market. It features ultra-strong hydro-formed aluminium top and down tubes, and has rectangular chain and seat stays which make the rear end feel like it's on rails.

Avent's sister company Bombshell are the makers of many BMX components, including Revolution wheelsets, Velocity cranks and the extremely popular F1 carbon fibre race forks – all of which are featured on this bike.

FRAME: AVENT TR7 CRUISER PRO XL
FORKS: BOMBSHELL F1
BARS: S&M 5.75" RACE
STEM: PROFILE RACE
HEADSET: TECHNIQUE
CRANKS: BOMBSHELL VELOCITY
SPROCKET: BOMBSHELL VELOCITY
PEDALS: NUKEPROOF PROTON
WHEELS: BOMBSHELL REVOLUTION
TYRES: INTENSE MICRO
SEAT: SDG TI FLY
SEAT POST: THOMSON ELITE
SEAT POST CLAMP: TECHNIQUE
BRAKE: SHIMANO DEORE
LEVER: SHIMANO DEORE
GRIPS: ODI

2010 STANDARD CUSTOM

SUBMITTED BY **KEN SPAULDING**

'Back when I brought on a partner to my high-end component company Zodiac Engineering,' says Ken Spaulding, 'we discussed building the ultimate bikes – throwing out all limitations and going with what we saw as the future of BMX.' The two then set about realizing exactly what they wanted from a BMX, including special touches such as turning brake mounts specific to Paul Moto brake arms.

Once Spaulding and his partner had figured out what they wanted, they contacted Rick Moliterno over at the Standard Byke Company, as he shares many of the same views as Zodiac Engineering when it comes to manufacturing and BMX in general. 'Being an American-made company like us, and constantly staying on the edge with materials and processes, we felt this would be a good fit,' says Spaulding. After a few emails back and forth, the details were nailed down, and here is the end result: a 9.5kg (21lb) bike that is fully capable of being ridden on the track, trails, park and street. With many of the parts being made at Zodiac Engineering, and the welded components being made by the Standard Byke Company, this bike is about as American as you can get.

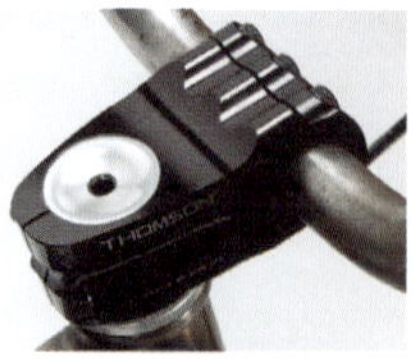

FRAME: CUSTOM STANDARD 21" TOP TUBE LENGTH, 14.00-14.38" CHAINSTAY LENGTH, 11.5" BOTTOM BRACKET HEIGHT, 8.5" STANDOVER HEIGHT C-C, 74.5 DEGREE HEADTUBE ANGLE, 71 DEGREE SEAT-TUBE ANGLE, 27.2MM SEAT TUBE ID, V-BRAKES ON THE SEAT STAYS (PAUL COMP MOTO BMX SPECIFIC MOUNTS), HIDDENSET SPEC HEADTUBE (TURNED TO 44MM OD), BB30 73MM BOTTOM BRACKET SHELL (PARAGON MACHINE WORKS), ENCLOSED REAR DROPOUTS, ADDITIONAL BRIDGES IN STAYS, STA GUSSET. FRAME PREP BY ATR
FORKS: CUSTOM STANDARD, ENCLOSED SLOTTED DROPOUTS 3/8", M24 X 1.5 THREAD
BARS: STANDARD STRIP, 7.75" X 28"
STEM: THOMSON BMX, SPACER REMOVED, COUNTERBORED
HEADSET: ZODIAC DUST CAP, NEEDLE BEARINGS
CRANKS: ODYSSEY (T) WOMBOLT ARMS 175MM, DUAL NON-DRIVE SIDE ARMS/BOLTS/WEDGES; SPINDLE: ZODIAC 25MM 7068, INTEGRATED DRIVE SIDE SPACER, SOCKET DRIVE; NON-DRIVE SIDE SPACER: ZODIAC 7068
SPROCKET: TREE SPLINE DRIVE LITE 36T, MODIFIED TO SOCKET DRIVE
PEDALS: ATOMLAB TRAILKING, SPINDLES SHORTENED, BROACHED FOR A 6MM HEX KEY
CHAIN: KMC 710SL, TIN COATED
HUBS: FRONT: ZODIACENG, FULL 7068, F1 CERAMIC - HYBRID CERAMIC BEARINGS, BLUESIX BIKES TITANIUM BOLTS; REAR: CHRIS KING, 12T, 36H, TITANIUM FEMALE 14MM AXLE, BLUESIX BIKES TITANIUM BOLTS
RIMS: ECLAT BONDI ROUND, 36H
TYRES: PROTOTYPE TIOGA
SEAT: FIT ECCD, KEVLAR COVER
SEAT POST: THOMSON MASTERPIECE 27.2MM
SEAT POST CLAMP: ZODIAC
BRAKE: PAUL MOTO BMX, PAD MOUNTS FLIPPED UPSIDE DOWN, ARM MOUNTS TURNED SPECIFICALLY FOR THE ARMS TO INCREASE STIFFNESS (ZODIAC)
LEVER: PAUL COMP LOVE
GRIPS: DIMENSION TRACK
EXTRAS: ZODIAC M24 X 1.5 PRELOAD, ZODIAC 7068 PLUG BAR-ENDS, NOKON BRAKE CABLE, PLAZMATIC BRAKE PADS WITH BLUESIX TITANIUM NUTS, MARWIUSA TITANIUM 14G SPOKES, MARWIUSA 7075 NIPPLES

2010 STANDARD TRLS 250L

SUBMITTED BY **DANIEL HARRIS**

Trails riding grew progressively throughout the 1990s and bikes of all shapes and sizes were used for it. If you were smooth you could ride a race bike over the trails as easily as you would a 1990s behemoth such as the STA 500 or S.O.B. from DK. However, trail-specific bikes were popping up quite commonly, including the S&M Dirt Bike, TNT's HWA Fong Daddy, the DK General Lee and the Standard Trail Boss.

When Robbie Morales left Standard, the company continued with the development of the Trail Boss but renamed it the Trails 250. Continuing with the themes of strength, build quality and saving weight using more modern materials, this frame has been a part of the Standard Legacy, under one guise or another, for many years now. It was later to become the 250L.

This bike's owner, Daniel Harris, explains: 'The Standard 250L is a modern update on the 250, but it's still 100% a 250. All the bolts are titanium on this build, as are the spokes, and the ball bearings have been replaced with ceramic bearings.' The bike also features a very limited Rob Ridge-made freecoaster rear hub (number one of three ever built). Ridge is a UK rider who rides for Standard.

FRAME: 250L 20.75" LITE
FORKS: UK
BARS: ALONE
STEM: ODYSSEY
HEADSET: ODYSSEY SEALED GYRO
CRANKS: MACNEIL CONJOINED
SPROCKET: STANDARD BYKES PROTOYPE 24T
PEDALS: KHE WITH TITANIUM AXLE
CHAIN: KHE
HUBS: FRONT: PROFILE MINI WITH CERAMIC BEARINGS; REAR: LIMITED-EDITION ROB RIDGE CUSTOM NANKAI BAMBOO FREECOASTER MACHINED INTO A PROFILE FREECOASTER HUB SHELL WITH CUSTOM TITANIUM INTERNALS AND CERAMIC BEARINGS
RIMS: ODYSSEY
TYRES: KHE 2.1
SEAT: MACNEIL
SEAT POST: MACNEIL
SEAT POST CLAMP: ODYSSEY
BRAKES: FRONT: ODYSSEY; REAR: FLY
LEVERS: ODYSSEY
GRIPS: ODI
EXTRAS: RAINBOW TITANIUM SPOKES, VARIOUS TITANIUM NUTS AND BOLTS

FRAME: INTENSE PODIUM
FORKS: SINZ ELITE CARBON PRO
BARS: SINZ
STEM: PROFILE ACOUSTIC, 53MM
HEADSET: SINZ INTERNAL
CRANKS: PROFILE RACE BOSS-LESS, 175
SPROCKET: PROFILE BOSS-LESS SPIDER, SINZ 44T CHAINRING
PEDALS: CRANK BOTHERS
CHAIN: SINZ
HUBS: SINZ IHUB
RIMS: SINZ ELITE PRO
TYRES: ITS HUSTLER 20 X 1.75
SEAT: THE ICON MINI
SEAT POST: SINZ
SEAT POST CLAMP: SINZ QR
BRAKE: SINZ, WITH SINZ COLOURED PADS
LEVER: SINZ
GRIPS: SINZ ELITE BOLT-ONS
EXTRAS: SINZ TRIPLE-BUTTED STRAIGHT-PULL SPOKES WITH ALLOY NIPPLES

2011 INTENSE PODIUM

SUBMITTED BY **TOBY HENDERSON**

A leading manufacturer of BMX racing frames, Intense BMX was founded (and is still run) by BMX legend Toby Henderson, a previous national and world champion in BMX. Intense manufacture high-end frames as well as a large range of complete BMX race bikes to cater for all ages and abilities.

Perhaps one of the most recognizable race frames on the market, the Intense Podium is at the technological forefront of frame design, with its top and down tubes being hydro-formed into their distinctive shapes (using full 6061 aluminium alloy). With well-considered geometry, the down tube is triple butted (leaving metal where it's needed and having less where it's not), for a flex-free ride while retaining strength and reducing weight. Other features include an integrated headtube, double-butted chainstays, triple-butted seat stays, CNC-machined dropouts and a total of 15 different frame sizes to choose from.

This particular bike has been custom painted and belongs to US Intense team rider Arielle Martin, the 2008 elite women's UCI Supercross World Cup champion.

FRAME: SPEED M-SERIES 20, M546
FORKS: SINZ ELITE CARBON PRO LITE, 20-MIL
BARS: SINZ
STEM: SINZ
HEADSET: SINZ INTERNAL
CRANKS: SINZ ELITE XXX, 175
SPROCKET: SINZ 44T
PEDALS: CRANK BOTHERS
CHAIN: SINZ
HUBS: SINZ 20-MIL IHUB
RIMS: SINZ ELITE PRO
TYRES: ITS MK2 20 X 1.75
SEAT: THE ICON PRO
SEAT POST: SINZ
SEAT POST CLAMP: SINZ QR
BRAKE: SINZ, WITH SINZ COLOURED PADS
LEVER: SINZ
GRIPS: THE BOLT-ONS
EXTRAS: SINZ ELITE XXX BOTTOM BRACKET, SINZ TRIPLE-BUTTED STRAIGHT-PULL SPOKES WITH ALLOY NIPPLES

2011 SPEED M-SERIES

SUBMITTED BY **TOBY HENDERSON**

BMX legend and now product visionary of VSI Products Toby Henderson has designed this integrated frame, fork and wheel system or 'rolling chassis' that he believes will have a lasting impact on the sport of BMX for decades to come. 'This is the first significant evolution in BMX frame design since the chromoly unicrown fork,' says Henderson. 'Our testing indicates that a racer will have a significant speed advantage out of the gate, down the straight and while cornering over other racers on frames with traditional axle configurations.'

Specially designed front and rear hubs with larger, hollow 20mm aluminium axles, combined with massive 32mm hub/dropout interfaces on the frame and forks, mean bikes built with these new rolling chassis are noticeably stiffer. The result: no noticeable flex and greater power transfer for faster gate starts and more precise handling. The hubs' straight-pull spoke design further boosts rigidity while making the wheels stronger, as straight-pull spokes are approximately 30% stronger than J-bend spokes, plus there are no hub flanges to break.

Speed bikes aren't available as complete builds, but as rolling chassis kits (including a Speed M-Series frame, Sinz Elite Stealth carbon fibre forks, iHub wheels, Sinz internal headset and Sinz stem), which are available in five sizes. The bike shown here belongs to former Speed team rider Nick Koehler.

2011
FBM STEADFAST

SUBMITTED BY **STEVE CRANDALL**

FRAME: FBM STEADFAST
FORKS: ODYSSEY
BARS: FBM BELMARS
STEM: FBM BOTTLENECK
HEADSET: FBM INTEGRATED
CRANKS: PROFILE
HUBS: PROFILE
GRIPS: FBM NICE MISO

BMX is lucky enough to have rider-owned companies all over the world, some are into winning the X Games and having the biggest team, some are race-specific, some offer great value for money and some are uncompromising on strength or build quality.

Fat Bald Men (FBM) makes bikes to the highest standards using modern materials with super-therm tubing and they come in a variety of shapes and sizes. It was one of the first companies to be running bikes with a sharper 75-degree headtube. The bike shown here, however, is Steve Crandall's very own personal ride, the Steadfast, which features a mellow 74-degree headtube angle and is light and fast. It's a perfect frame to take to the trails or hit your local park with – pegless, of course.

2011
DELUXE TECH II

SUBMITTED BY **MARK NOBLE**

Deluxe BMX was founded in 2008 by Mark Noble, ex-editor of *Ride UK BMX* magazine. Noble has been in the industry for almost as long as there's been an industry in the UK, and has seen pretty much all there is to see.

Deluxe is a simple and stylish brand and its bikes reflect Noble's attitude towards BMXing. From the early roots of BMX, when kids rode their bikes around the back yard and on dirt ramps in the 1970s and 1980s, to present-day trails with 6-metre (20-foot) gaps, the company seems to be able to encapsulate the notion of having fun on bikes through a clean but well-informed design aesthetic.

This is a 2011 Tech II frame, Noble comments. 'It's a mix of what we make, to be honest. When it came to designing the frame I just used a combination of feedback from everyone on the team, along with years and years of experience spent riding, testing, measuring, and analyzing pretty much every single BMX frame that came to market while I was editing BMX magazines. I saw a lot of frames and bikes during those decades, so I had a pretty reasonable idea of what to make when it came to our own frames, and how the geometry works and affects the ride and balance of a frame. So, when it comes to a balanced, predictable, fast and fun bike to ride, what we have here works. Using the latest tech and butting profiles for chromoly tubing, we kept the technology and strength hidden within the frame, giving a no-fuss super-clean exterior, and a high-quality frame build. That's what we're all about, and I couldn't be happier with this bike. There's something amazingly satisfying [about] riding a bike you've designed.'

FRAME: DELUXE TECH II, SIZE L 20.7"
FORKS: KIS FEMALE AXLE SPECIFIC
BARS: DELUXE L-SIZE WITH BAR-END EXTENDERS
STEM: DELUXE F-LITE
CRANKS: HARO THREE-PIECE
SPROCKET: DELUXE POMPOM, 25T
PEDALS: DELUXE F-LITE
HUBS: FRONT, DELUXE F-LITE HUB; REAR F-LITE CASSETTE HUB, 9T
RIMS: SUN
TYRES: FRONT: ODYSSEY AITKEN KNOBBLY; REAR: ODYSSEY DIRT PATH
SEAT: DELUXE SUPERLIGHT
SEAT POST: SINZ
SEAT POST CLAMP: DELUXE F-LITE
BRAKE: DIA-COMPE
LEVER: AFFIX
GRIPS: DELUXE SHOVELHANDS
EXTRAS: FLY BIKES SPANISH BOTTOM BRACKET

LIKE MOST COLLECTORS, IT USUALLY STARTS AS A MILD INTEREST IN REVISITING YOUR YOUTH AND RELIVING THE GOOD TIMES, MAYBE BUYING A BIKE OR TWO YOU WANTED AS A KID. YOU GET INTO THE SCENE AND THEN IT SNOWBALLS...

INTERVIEW WITH A COLLECTOR: MARK JAMES

Location:
Hull, UK

What is your connection to BMX?
Like most collectors around my age (I'm 36), it usually starts as a mild interest in revisiting your youth and reliving the good times, maybe buying a bike or two you wanted as a kid. You get into the scene and then it snowballs...

When did you start collecting pristine old-school bikes?
I got introduced to eBay in 2003, typed in some random words and saw a 1985 Haro Master frame and forks and had it as a gift for Christmas.

How many bikes do you have?
Just counted 28. I had about 80 in the last six years, but they come and go, some bought out of idle curiosity but mostly what I have now is filtered down to my favourites. I've tried to have a good rounded collection but there's room for improvement and change. I'm always tweaking.

How and where are they stored?
I have a room dedicated to them, tall white walls to hang [them] on and a display on the floor.

Do you build them to showcase?
I do, it's part of our calendar in collecting circles to have a few secret builds every year [that] you pull out of the bag to take to the RadBMX meets or to build for the Bike of the Year contests on the forums.

What's your holy grail?
It was the Hutch Pro Star and probably still is. I guess it's something you haven't got is your holy grail, something elusive you're chasing. The matching Trick Star was last year's chase, the holy grail became to have the pair, that has been satisfied now. It doesn't always have to be about the money builds though, original untouched examples of more modest bikes can win me over. The Torker 280X (see page 56) is a good example. I could go on, there [are] too many. Perfect unrestored examples of whatever it is, that's the holy grail.

When you've been collecting for a number of years you end up with a stash of spares, it annoys the guys new to the hobby, but it makes sense if you're into collecting for the long haul. It makes it easier and cheaper to start a new build when you've got a stash of bits to get a head start. The JMC Shadow is a perfect example, no labour of love or big hunt for parts, just delve around a few boxes, get a spanner out and it's done.

JMC SHORT STANDARD

SE RACING PK RIPPER

HUTCH TRICK STAR

HUTCH TRICK STAR AND PRO STAR

JMC SHADOW

GT TEAM SERIES

I KEEP THE BIKES ON DISPLAY AT THE BMX ADDICTS MUSEUM, A 2,000-SQUARE-FOOT LOCATION IN MIAMI.

INTERVIEW WITH A COLLECTOR: JUAN MATTOS

Location:
Miami, Florida, USA

When did you start collecting?
June 2007

What is your connection to BMX?
I've ridden a BMX since I was 8 years old and was the 1984 Under 16 Expert National Champion and 1986 A Pro National Champion in Bogota, Colombia, South America. I still ride street a couple of times a week.

How many bikes have you got?
At one point I had around 100 bikes, which I kept on display at the BMX Addicts Museum, a 2,000-square-foot location in Miami (pictured). However, many of the bikes I used to own have traded hands during the course of 2010/2011 and most of my valuable pieces were sold to a very good friend of mine in Australia. The very few pieces I have kept are now at my home as there's no need for the huge set up I used to have.

How did your collection start? Did you just see a bike and think 'I gotta have that'?
Actually, the collecting started because of Sebastian, my 8-year-old son. I've always had plans of riding a bike with him, I've always wanted to get him into BMX, but after a few visits to the stores, I couldn't find a single bicycle that looked right for me (bikes today are strange, the seat is too low, the tyres are too fat and they are even heavier)... So it occurred to me to try and find something from back in the day. I sat on the computer, typed 'BMX old school' in the eBay search window and got 9,000 plus listings... I was hooked.

One day in June 2007 (the exact same day of my birthday) I completed my very first bike assembly, a 1985 Haro Master. Once I built that one I just couldn't stop. I have been lucky enough to be able to acquire a few collections in a relatively short period of time, but what sincerely humbles me is the good friends and the super cool people I have been able to meet through collecting. I try to support the vintage community as much as I can by helping various dedicated vintage BMX events and have a couple of sites up online. One was set up to share images of all the bikes I have built and collected (bmx-addicts.com), and another to help BMX enthusiasts around the world to connect, bmxspace.com.

GARY TURNER

COOK BROS. RACING

GJS BIG TUBE

GT MINI

SKYWAY TA CRUISER

SCHWINN STING

WE DIALLED OUR BIKES UP A BIT, ADDED SUPER-SKINNY PEGS, DICE CAPS, FAKE CW BARS AND AERO SEATS.

INTERVIEW WITH A COLLECTOR: CHRIS LAW

Location:
Boston, Massachusetts, USA

What is your connection to BMX?
My relationship with BMX started in '81–'82, when I was about ten. Up until that point I'd been riding around on a yellow Raleigh Boxer. It was a cool little bike, and was styled like a BMX, but I'd finally outgrown it and all my friends on the estate were either riding Raleigh Grifters or Raleigh Choppers.

Christmas was coming and my mum took me to her friend's shop, a weird place that stocked all types of stuff – TVs, stereos and other things. I walked in and only remember seeing one bike in there, which luckily enough for me was a brand new blue and yellow Raleigh Tuff Burner. Result!

I grew up with a good bunch of lads, all from similar backgrounds, and we ended up with BMXs (as did many kids [at] that time). BMX was huge, the new thing, and we loved it. We never had a real track or anything decent near us, just a couple of home-made jumps on some wasteland. We dialled our bikes up a bit, added super-skinny pegs, dice caps, fake CW bars and Aero seats.

Those were cool times, but after a few years most of the lads evolved onto road bikes – Peugeots, Raleigh Records, etc. They were OK, but I still loved BMX, and that started my next wave of interest around '86–'87. I acquired a white DP Firebird Freestyler, with white tyres, A'ME grips and an ACS Hollow Bolt stem. It went through various colour changes (hand-sprayed in the shed), and I used to save up and order parts using the forms in magazines.

I eventually moved on, got a motorbike, a car, a girlfriend, etc. But then around '91 I got the buzz again after meeting up with an old BMX friend (and semi-pro rider) Darren Gascoyne. I used to deliver post to Darren's house and remember seeing all his stickers on his bedroom window: Invert Magazine, Vision Street Wear and others. This was my third wave of BMX. I used to go out street riding as I loved all the old Anarchic Adjustment ads, etc. I loved that era and that attitude that went with it, and regularly drove my Mini (packed with people and bikes) up to Stevenage skate park.

A love of BMX has always stayed with me, but now being a father of three, I don't get out as much as I'd like. I ride my 26er to work everyday, and take my 24s out with the nippers (on their rippers) and try and teach them how to jump off curbs etc. I still get the thrill of putting bikes together, dialling them up and generally geeking out.

When did you start collecting bikes?
I'm not really a collector, just a hoarder I think.

How and where are they stored?
In the basement/garage.

Do you build them to showcase?
Not really, I like to look at them, I get enjoyment from what parts I use, how they work together, what the theme is, etc. I'm a footwear designer by trade, so it's how the pieces make up a whole. Colour is also very important, as well as surface texture.

What's your holy grail?
I would say a grey/white Skyway Street Beat with grey Skyways and white Comp ST tyres.

SE RACING QUADANGLE 24

SE RACING OM FLYER 26

KAPPA K24

ADIDAS ORIGINALS KAPPA K24

SUPERCROSS MX26

PASHLEY TV SERIES 24

INTERVIEW WITH MARK NOBLE OF DELUXE BMX

Location:
Dorchester, Dorset, UK

When and how did you first get in to BMX?
I'd always loved bikes, turning them in to pseudo-MX type bikes, jumping logs and whatnot around our garden when I was younger with my brother Chris. Skids and wheelies and all that. So when BMX bikes arrived on the scene I jumped in with both feet, it was perfect. My dad brought back a copy of BMX Action magazine from one of his States trips, and that was it, I was hooked.

What is your favourite bike?
Perhaps my first BMX bike, a Falcon Black Arrow 2000 in burgundy with black parts and gold graphics, or maybe the Skyway Street Beat I won the Tizer Worlds on in 1988 (I'd like to know where that bike is now!). Actually, the Deluxe bike I'm riding right now (see page 145) is my personal favourite I think. Perhaps I do wish I'd owned a black Haro Sport of the Brian Blyther era, complete with a tennis ball wedged in the front wheel spokes.

You were the editor of Ride BMX magazine for a long time; did you ever have your doubts about the stability of the BMX industry?
In a nutshell, I have edited BMX magazines since I was around 17 years old – from 1987 until June 2008. That's over 20 years running BMX magazines – so I've seen a hell of a lot of change and trends come and go during those two decades in publishing. Fascinating times as well. We endured huge dips in the popularity of the sport when there was barely a handful of BMX shops in the whole of the UK, and when the number of riders involved was at an all-time low. But we always stuck with making the magazine because we knew it was vital for the scene and we just loved it. Financially it really didn't make any sense at times, but then as long as we were making BMX magazines and enjoying BMX as a whole, I really didn't care.

BMX now is possibly stronger than ever, as riders who grew up during the heyday are now by-and-large running the industry. Riders now own and run companies, bike brands, parts brands, bike shops, mail-order shops, clothing companies, shoe brands, skateparks and even their own print and media operations. Experienced riders running the right parts of BMX can only be a good thing. If you've been into BMX a ton, you should inherently understand it and at least care about it – which gives you a leg up on the people who are in the industry purely for the money.

Which bikes do you currently have in your collection?
I have a bunch of frames - a Vector Mark2 which I won in one of the first UK freestyle contests back in 1986; a Champion Pro; a white Hutch Trick Star, Craig Campbell's No.3 Prolite, a Diamondback Mini, a Vincent Frames Freestyler and some mk1 Deluxe frames, among others.

Full bikes I have include a mid-90s S&M Dirt Bike built with a random collection of old parts (see page 100); an original mk1 UK-spec Haro Sport just as it was when it popped out the box; a replica Mongoose Supergoose, a Federal Steven Hamilton; and a 2011 Deluxe Tech2 built up with a bunch of our finest Deluxe products.

Which single manufacturer do you think has had the greatest effect on the BMX industry over the past 40 years?
Bike company wise, quite probably S&M Bikes. From forming a rider-owned company and showing people that it can be done, to heralding US-made, in-house construction, to its can-do attitude and drive – I think Chris Moeller at S&M has really been a huge inspiration to many rider-owned companies today.

What makes Deluxe tick?
Designing product, having it made, working with Chris on the graphics and the guys on the team, and the ads and the videos and the creative people who get involved – it's great. And receiving an email out of the blue from a guy who rides our bikes and just wrote to say how much he loves it, well, that really makes my day. Really inspirational, and it all drives us to make things better.

MANUFACTURERS' GLOSSARY

2-Hip
www.2hip.com

Avent Cycles
No dedicated web page at the time of writing

Blue Max
www.vintagemongoose.com/products/bluemax.php

Brian Curtis (now Curtis)
www.curtisbikes.co.uk

Brooklyn Machine Works
www.brooklynmachineworks.com

Cook bros.
www.cookbros.com

CW
www.cw-racing.com

Deluxe BMX
www.deluxebmx.com

DG
www.dgbmx.wordpress.com

Diamond Back (now Diamondback)
www.diamondback.co.uk

DK
www.dkbicycles.com

DP Racing
www.dpfirebird.co.uk

Eastern Bikes
www.easternbikes.com

FBM Bike Co.
www.fbmbmx.com

Fit Bike Co.
www.fitbikeco.com

Fly Bikes
www.flybikesbmx.com

Free Agent
www.freeagentbmx.com

G-Boy
No dedicated web page at the time of writing

GJS
No dedicated web page at the time of writing

GT
www.gtbicycles.com

Haro Bikes
www.harobikes.com

Hoffman Bikes
www.hoffmanbikes.com

Hutch
www.hutchbmx.com

Intense BMX
www.intensebmx.com

JAG
www.jagbmx.com

JMC (Jim Melton Cyclery)
www.jmcbmx.wordpress.com/about

Kappa
www.kappastore.com

Kawasaki BMX
www.bmxnonstop.com/oldschool/kawasaki/index.html

Kuwahara
www.kuwahara-bike.com

MacNeil
www.macneilbmx.com

Metal Bikes
www.metalbikesbmx.com

Mongoose
www.mongoose.com

Mosh (a division of Giant BMX, 1996-2003)
www.ridegiantbmx.com

Nomura
No dedicated web page at the time of writing

Pashley
www.pashley.co.uk

Patterson
No dedicated web page at the time of writing

Pro Neck
No dedicated web page at the time of writing

Profile
www.profileracing.com

Quamen
www.quamenbikes.com

Raleigh
www.raleigh.co.uk

Red Line (now Redline)
www.redlinebicycles.com

Rickman
No dedicated web page at the time of writing

Robinson
No dedicated web page at the time of writing

Roger Decoster
www.vintagemongoose.com/products/decoster.php

S&M
www.sandmbikes.com

Schauff
www.schauff.de

Schwinn
www.schwinn.com

SE Racing
www.sebikes.com

Skyway
www.skywaywheels.com

Speed
www.speed-bicycles.com

Standard Byke Company
www.standardbyke.com

Sunday
www.sundaybikes.com

Supercross
www.supercrossbmx.com

Terrible One
www.terribleone.com

TNT
No dedicated web page at the time of writing

Torker
www.torkerusa.com

VDC
www.vorisdixon.com

Webco
No dedicated web page at the time of writing

WeThePeople
www.wethepeoplebmx.de

Y-3
www.y-3store.com

CONTRIBUTORS' GLOSSARY

Name: Joe Alder
Location: Maryland, USA
Age: 40
Occupation: Engineer
Bikes included: Standard Tao

Name: Rob Anderman
Location: London, UK
Age: 39
Occupation: Stay-at-home dad
Bikes included: S&M .38 Special Cruiser

Name: Christopher Appoldt
Location: New York, USA
Age: 40
Occupation: Editor, photographer
Bikes included: Hutch Pro Racer, SE Racing Quadangle

Name: Joe Avedesian
Location: New York, USA
Age: 44
Occupation: Brooklyn Machine Works founder and company owner
Bikes included: Brooklyn Machine Works Pooky Cruiser
www.brooklynmachineworks.com

Name: Jim Bauer
Location: California, USA
Age: 31
Occupation: Art director
Bikes included: Metal Rebel Contender
www.odysseybmx.com

Name: Iain Bowden
Location: Glasgow, UK
Age: 39
Occupation: Buildings standards surveyor
Bikes included: DP Firebird Freestyler

Name: Harrison Boyce
Location: New York, USA
Age: 27
Occupation: Creative director
Bikes included: MacNeil Whitton
www.macneilbmx.com
www.defgrip.net

Name: John Buultjens
Location: Melbourne, Australia
Age: 39
Occupation: CEO Pilgrim BMX
Bikes included: Haro Freestyler
www.pilgrimbmx.com

Name: Matthew Cowle
Location: Isle of Man, UK
Age: 31
Occupation: Labourer
Bikes included: KHE Premium Lagger

Name: Steve Crandell
Location: New York, USA
Age: 35
Occupation: Founder/owner FBM Bike Co.
Bikes included: FBM Steadfast
www.fbmbmx.com

Name: Adam Dawson
Bikes included: Hoffman Condor

Name: Nathan Van Driel
Location: Alberta, Canada
Age: 28
Occupation: Graphic designer/photographer
Bikes included: Terrible One Progression

Name: Dean Druce
Location: New South Wales, Australia
Age: 36
Occupation: Civil engineer
Bikes included: Haro Team Master, Haro Team Sport, Hoffman Big Daddy

Name: Duane Franklin
Location: Hawaii, USA
Age: 36
Occupation: Store manager
Bikes included: Robinson Pro Team

Name: Michael Gamstetter
Location: California, USA
Age: 45
Occupation: Marketing manager/product designer
Bikes included: GJS A-Frame, JMC Black Shadow, Profile Champ Pro, Schwinn Scambler

Name: Brendan Green
Bikes included: TNT HWA Fong Daddy

Name: Dave Hall
Location: South Yorkshire, UK
Age: 36
Occupation: Contracts manager
Bikes included: Raleigh Aero Pro Burner, Raleigh Tuff Burner
www.burnerworld.co.uk

Name: Daniel Harris
Location: Suffolk, UK
Age: 40
Occupation: BMX restoration, exhibitions and displays
Bikes included: Standard Shorty, Standard STA 500, Standard Trail Boss, Standard TRLS 250L

Name: Toby Henderson
Location: California, USA
Age: 48
Occupation: Ex-pro BMX Rider
Bikes included: Intense Podium, Speed M-Series
www.intensebmx.com
www.speed-bicycles.com

Name: Glynn Hicks
Location: Brisbane, Australia
Age: 42
Occupation: Ex-pro BMX Rider
Bikes included: BMX Products Blue Max, JAG BMX Café Racer, JAG BMX Team, JMC Standard Long, Redline Proline, Roger DeCoster (Short),

Name: Jeremy Hicks
Location: Winchester, UK
Age: 39
Occupation: Business services architect
Bikes included: Avent TR7 Cruiser

Name: Chris Hilton
Location: London, UK
Age: 35
Occupation: Creative director
Bikes included: Skyway Street Beat

Name: Dave Hudson
Location: California, USA
Age: The over-40 club
Occupation: Engineering project coordinator
Bikes included: 2-Hip Bikes Pork, Fit Bike Aitken 3.5

Name: Woody Itson
Location: California, USA
Age: 40
Occupation: Ex-pro BMX Rider
Bikes included: Hutch Trick Star, Redline Proline, Torker Freestyle Prototype

Name: Mark James
Location: Hull, UK
Age: 36
Occupation: DJ and bar owner
Bikes included: GT Team Series, Hutch Pro Star, Hutch Trick Star, JMC Shadow, JMC Short Standard, Kuwahara KZ-1, Mongoose Motomag, SE Racing PK Ripper, Skyway TA, Torker 280X

Name: Geoffrey Jordan
Location: Manitoba, Canada
Age: 31
Occupation: Army
Bikes included: Fly Bikes Pantera

Name: Ravi Kajla
Location: London, UK
Age: 33
Occupation: Experiential account handler
Bikes included: Rickman Freestyler

Name: Chris Law
Location: Boston, Massachusetts, USA
Age: 38
Occupation: Design director
Bikes included: adidas Originals Kappa K24, Kappa K24, Pashley TV Series 24, SE Racing OM Flyer 26, SE Racing Quadangle 24, Supercross MX26, Supercross Evo 24

Name: Gavin Lucas
Location: London, UK
Age: 34
Occupation: Author, blogger, journalist
Bikes included: Skyway Street Beat

Name: Juan Mattos
Location: Miami, USA
Age: 41
Occupation: Wholesale and distribution
Bikes included: Big Tube, Cook Bros. Racing, Cook Bros. 'S' Bar, CW California Freestyler, CW Phaze 1 Cruiser, CW Phaze 1 (Team Issue), DG-1, Diamond Back Silver Streak, Diamond Back Turbo, Diamond Back Turbo Pit Bike, Free Agent Free Flight Freestyle, FMF Team Bike, Gary Turner, G-Boy, GJS Freestyler Prototype, GT Mini, Hutch LiL Holeshot, Hutch The Judge, Hutch XL 24, JMC Cruiser, JMC XP-2, Nomura, Pro Neck National Pro Standard, Redline Monoshock, Redline 'Palfreyman' Looptail, Redline PL-20 Carrera, Redline RL-20 Pro-Styler, Redline Squareback, Schwinn Sting, SE Racing Floval Flyer, SE Racing JU-6, SE Racing OM Flyer, Skyway TA Cruiser, Two Wheeler Stroker II, VDC Changa, VDC Changa Freestyle
www.bmx-addicts.com

Name: Steve Mitchell
Location: Colorado, USA
Age: 36
Occupation: Software engineer
Bikes included: DK S.O.B.

Name: Lee Morris
Location: North Yorkshire, UK
Age: 43
Occupation: Maintenance engineer
Bikes included: Kuwahara ET

Name: Mark Noble
Location: Dorset, UK
Age: 43
Occupation: Bike brand owner/journalist
Bikes included: Deluxe Tech II, S&M Dirt Bike
www.deluxebmx.com

Name: Kyle Pucek
Location: Wisconsin, USA
Age: 35
Occupation: Property management
Bikes included: Fly Bikes Tierra, Sunday Funday

Name: Scott Rekdal
Location: Washington, DC, USA
Age: 37
Occupation: Assistant Vice President of Marketing, NDIA
Bikes included: Hutch Trick Star

Name: Gary Sansom
Location: Portland, USA
Age: 46
Occupation: Webmaster at BMX Museum
Bikes included: DK General Lee, Hoffman Evel Knievel
www.bmxmuseum.com

Name: Jan Schauff
Location: Remagen/Rhine, Germany
Age: 47
Occupation: Engineer
Bikes included: Schauff Flatland Prototype

Name: Marc Seeman
Location: Iowa USA
Age: 25
Occupation: Student/mechanic
Bikes included: Fit Bike Series 1, Schwinn Stingray

Name: Jurjen Semeijn
Location: Amsterdam, The Netherlands
Age: 34
Occupation: Entrepreneur, artist
Bikes included: Mosh Method

Name: Josh Smith
Location: Illinois, USA
Age: 40
Occupation: EMT student
Bikes included: Standard Tao

Name: Ken Spaulding
Location: Orange, California, USA
Age: 26
Occupation: Machinist
Bikes included: Quamen Clad G8, Standard Custom, Terrible One SFA
www.zodiaceng.com

Name: Andreas Stevens
Location: California, USA
Age: 40
Occupation: DJ/producer
Bikes included: Gary Littlejohn Sidehack, Patterson PR240 Cruiser, Webco Replica

Name: Joseph Stevenson
Location: Sheffield, UK
Age: 37
Occupation: Actor
Bikes included: Eastern Grim Reaper, S&M Challenger, S&M Holmes, S&M Next Generation Holmes, S&M Sabbath, S&M XLAF, Standard 125 Motocross, Terrible One Custom Paul B

Name: Carl Turner
Location: Shropshire, UK
Age: 41
Occupation: Designer
Bikes included: GT Performer

Name: Chris Willet
Location: Daventry, UK
Age: 36
Occupation: Company director
Bikes included: Mongoose DMC

Name: Nick Wilson
Location: Bristol, UK
Age: 41
Occupation: Recoveries manager
Bikes included: Curtis Pro

Name: Michael de Wit
Location: California, USA
Age: 33
Occupation: Art director
Bikes included: Kawasaki BX200, JMC Short

RESOURCES

Build Your Own BMX

Alans BMX
www.alansbmx.com

C4 Labs
www.c4labspc.com

Restoration Nation
www.bmxrestorations.com

RetrospectBMX.com
www.retrospectbmx.com

Source BMX
www.sourcebmx.com

Vert-Ego
www.vert-ego.com

Volt BMX
www.voltbmx.com

Forums/Memorabilia/History

23 Mag
www.23mag.com

Bicross.org
www.bicross.org

Bikeguide.org
www.bikeguide.org

BMX Action Online
www.bmxactiononline.com

BMX Addicts
www.bmx-addicts.com

BMX Feed
www.bmxfeed.com

BMX Forum
www.bmx-forum.com

BMX Hobbies
www.bmxhobbies.com

BMXmuseum
www.bmxmuseum.com

BMX Plus!
www.bmxplusmag.com

BMX Restoration
www.bmxrestoration.co.uk

BMX Talk
www.bmxtalk.com

Burnerworld
www.burnerworld.co.uk

Colored Tuffs/PlanetBMX
www.coloredtuffs.com

Defgrip
www.blog.defgrip.net

Global-Flat.com
www.global-flat.com

Holeshot
www.holeshotbmx.blogspot.com

HaroBMXcollector.com
www.harobmxcollector.com

HaroFreestyler.com
www.harofreestyler.com

Jamie's Kuwahara site
www.dreamgate.ne.jp/kuwahara

LeastMost
www.leastmost.com

Old School BMX
www.oldschoolbmx.wordpress.com

PK Ripper Heaven
www.pkripperheaven.com

RadBMX
www.radbmx.co.uk

The Come Up
www.thecomeupbmx.net

University of BMX
www.universityofbmx.com

Vital BMX
www.vitalbmx.com

Vintage BMX
www.vintagebmx.com

Vintage Mongoose
www.vintagemongoose.com

Magazines

BMX Action
www.oldschoolmags.com/BMX_Action.html

BMX Plus!
www.oldschoolmags.com/BMX_Plus.html

BMXtra
www.bmxtra.com

CaseBMX
www.casebmx.com

Classic BMX
www.classicbmxmag.com

Cream
www.myspace.com/creambmxmagazine

Dig BMX
www.digbmx.mpora.com

Fastlane BMX
www.fastlanebmxmag.com

FatBMX
www.fatbmx.com

Freestylin'
www.oldschoolmags.com/Freestylin_.html

Holeshot
www.holeshotbmx.blogspot.com

RideUK BMX
www.rideukbmx.mpora.com

Soul BMX
www.soulbmxmag.com

Transworld BMX
www.bmx.transworld.net

Zwanzig Zoll
www.zwanzig-zoll.de

Films

Joe Kidd On A Sting-Ray: The History of BMX
www.joekidonastingray.com

Stompin Stu Thomsen:
The Story of BMX Legend Stu Thomsen
www.stompinstu.com

The Birth of Big Air
(Mat Hoffman documentary)
30for30.espn.com/film/birth-of-big-air.html

E.T. The Extra Terrestrial
www.en.wikipedia.org/wiki/E.T._the_
Extra-Terrestrial

RAD
www.en.wikipedia.org/wiki/Rad_(film)

BMX Bandits
www.en.wikipedia.org/wiki/BMX_Bandits_(film)

Video and Film Resources

BMX Movie Database
www.bmxmdb.com

Action Sports Videos/BMX
www.actionsportsvideos.com/bmx.html

Sanctioning/Governing Bodies

American Bicycle Association (ABA)
www.ababmx.com

British Cycling
www.britishcycling.org.uk/bmx

National Bicycle League (NBL)
www.nbl.org

Union Cycliste Internationale
www.uci.ch

INDEX

Page numbers in **bold** refer to illustrations

Acknowledgements

Thank you to all the riders and collectors who responded so positively to the call for entries for this book, sending images and info about their BMX bikes from around the world.

Particular thanks must also go to our tireless picture researcher Ida Riveros, and to Jo Lightfoot, Sarah Batten and Donald Dinwiddie at Laurence King for their patience and support.

Sincere thanks also to:
Eliza Williams, Mark Sinclair, Patrick Burgoyne, Paul Pensom and all at Creative Review magazine, Leo Sandino-Taylor, Simon Wainwright and all at Nike, Tim Pateman, Karen Day, Chris Gray, Dean Druce, Seb Lester, Johann Chan, Scott Rekdal, Iain Bowden, Woody Itson, Juan Mattos, Glynn Hicks, Mark Noble, Steve Crandell, Chris Hilton, Ravi Kajla, Leo Walton, Leo Cackett, John Dye, Kevin Freel and all at Volt BMX, Scot Breithaupt, Glynn Hicks, Darren Wood, Jim Melton, John DeBruin, Alex, James and Rudy Joyce, Emily Haynes, Andy Ruffell, Ben Joy, Chris Overholser, Dave Hall, Gary Sansom, Harrison Boyce, James Fairbank, Joseph Stevenson, Mark James, Jason Eley, Jurjen Semeijn, Chris Law, Mike Klein, AustinFromNEW, Tom Hand, Will Kemp, Decoy BMX, Epaminondas Onoufriou, Tu Hoang, Nick Foot, Brendan Wavish, Colin Dower and the FBRS

Special thanks to Emma, Stanley and Sukey Gale,
Cressida, Woody and Vincent Robinson,
and to Ravi, the future Mrs Lucas

Credits

Cover: Photo: Leo Cackett
Pages 4-5 Photo: Kai Kuusisto
Page 10 Image courtesy of the American Bicycle Association
Page 11 All images by Kai Kuusisto except park image by Gareth Howell
Pages 14-15 Image courtesy of Scot Breithaupt
Page 17 Image courtesy of Scot Breithaupt
Page 18–19 Images courtesy of Scot Breithaupt, The Cycling Sports Group, vintagemongoose.com and Redline Bicycles
Page 38-39 Photo: Lee Reynolds by Mark Noble
Page 41 ET photo: Universal/The Kobal Collection
Pages 42-43 Images courtesy of Jan Schauff, Skyway, The Cycling Sports Group, Mark Noble, Andy Ruffell and vintagemongoose.com
Page 83 Photo: Dean Pellerzi
Page 87 Photo: www.studiomodaphotography.com
Page 89 Photo: www.studiomodaphotography.com
Pages 90-91 Photo: Getty Images
Page 93 Photo: Getty Images
Pages 94-95 Images courtesy of Mark Noble
Page 95 Rick Moliterno image courtesy of the Standard Byke Company
Page 97 Photo: www.studiomodaphotography.com
Page 106 Image by Jeff Walters
Page 109 Image by vndrl.com
Pages 112-113 Photo: George Marshall
Page 115 Top image: Getty Images; bottom image: Getty Images
Page 116 Jim Bauer image by Ricky Adam
Pages 116 Top left image: Gareth Howell; top right image: Keith Romanowski; second row, left image: George Marshall
Pages 116-117 Images courtesy of the American Bicycle Association
Page 117 Jim Bauer image by Justin Kosman
Page 117 Top right image: Kai Kuusisto; third row, right image: Gareth Howell
Pages 121 and 137 Images by Alison Hudson
Page 150 Chris Law image courtesy of Errol Photography